**Learn Korean with Classic Short Stories Beginner
(Downloadable Audio and English-Korean Bilingual Dual Text)**

ISBN 979-11-88195-73-2

Hye-min Choi

Download Audio Files From **newampersand.com/STORY**

Appendix - Quick Korean Lessons For Beginners

Download Audio Files From newampersand.com/STORY

Why Study With Korean Folk Tales?

Whether you're a K-pop fan, a Korean drama fan, or an aspiring Korean studies expert, learning Korean with stories is a great way not only to obtain the skills necessary for communication but to develop a deep understanding of the culture and ideology in which the language is used. Without knowing the cultural and historical background of a word, an expression, and a story, you won't be able to appreciate the subtle differences in nuance because you won't accurately understand the context in which they are used.

With folk tales, which combine the linguistic aspect of the language and the cultural and historical aspect, you can learn to understand grammar, the expressions Korean people use, and expand your Korean vocabulary. It also allows you to take a peek into the traditional ideology of Korean people so you can understand why Koreans do what they do. So let's take a journey to the olden days of Korea, and by the time we're back, you will also gain a thorough insight into Korean culture. But first, here is some useful information that will help you hit the ground running.

Hojakdo 호작도 **(Painting of Tiger, Magpie, and Pine Tree)**

Bansangdo, 반상도 Yangban (the nobles) and Commoners by Kim Deuk-sin (1754-1822)

Traditional Korean Ideology (Yugyo and Shamanism) Found In Folk Tales

Korea embraced Confucianism, or *yugyo* 유교 in Korean, developed by the Chinese philosopher Confucius, as their core philosophy as early as in the Three Kingdoms Period (57 BC – 668 AD), reaching its zenith during the Joseon Dynasty (1392-1897). As time passed, it gradually evolved into something more than an ideology. It became a civilization that governs the national system, politics, as well as the law and order. Its fundamental elements are **filial piety, loyalty, hierarchy, and obedience**, and they are the themes that repeatedly appear in the folk tales you're about to go through in the coming chapters (as a matter of fact, you can find the traits in modern-day Korean dramas or movies), so be on the lookout for them!

However, the modernization efforts in the 19th century caused the existing *yugyo* order to collapse considerably because Korean reformists blamed the misinterpreted and often abused *yugyo* customs for falling behind other advanced countries. Some of the examples include overly strict hierarchy, looking down on commerce and favoring scholars, patriarchal society, and nepotism.

For this reason, in modern-day Korea, *yugyo* purists are seen as outdated, and Koreans have been effectively maintaining a society built upon the core *yugyo* values through accepting and making necessary changes.

What Traditional Korean Families Looked Like

Traditionally, the Korean family has been a patrilocal stem family (i.e., a man remains to live in his father's house after reaching maturity and brings his wife to live with his family while daughters had to leave the natal house when they marry), and it was typical to see large families composed of multi-generations, including the grandparents, their eldest son and his wife, and their children (as an agricultural society, multi-children was the norm to supply labor force).

As for the hierarchy within the family, at the top are the males in descending order of age, largely due to the two major principles of *yugyo*: male shall dominate female and elder shall dominate the younger. Also, because only a son could continue the family line, it led to the son-preference.

Among the male children, the eldest, *jangnam* 장남 was considered the major pillar of the family and received preferential treatment, such as inheriting most, if not all, of the family estates. At the same time, however, he had to live with and look after their parents after getting married and was responsible for holding a *jesa* 제사 (ancestral rites) ceremony after their parents passed away.

For females, despite their lower status and limited roles, they were the object of reverence and respect. As wives, they were in charge of the family finance and domestic matters, and as mothers, the education of their children. The female children did not receive a systematic *yugyo* education, but mothers taught them to internalize *yugyo* virtues granted to women, as well as the role of a woman by learning household chores from an early age. From childhood, there were different educational processes and roles for boys and girls.

Shamanism

Traditionally, Koreans have believed in shamanism along with Buddhism. They believed there were divine beings governing nature, such as mountains and seas, as well as spirits in old objects. In addition, Koreans thought it was up to absolute beings in heaven to decide human life, death, reward, and punishment. Through these beliefs, Koreans thought that everything in life happens according to the providence of nature, and they have to adapt to the given environment, do their best, and live a good life, or heaven would punish them.

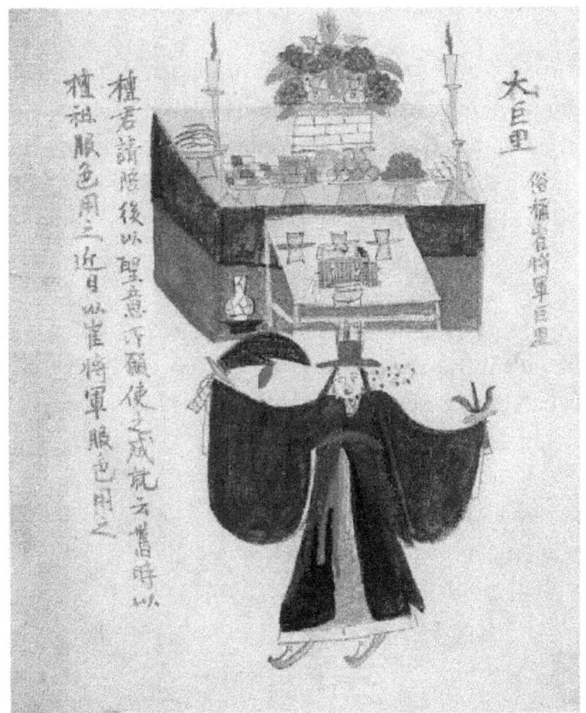

An illustration from *mudangnaeryeok* 무당내력, a compilation of the traditional Korean shaman exorcism methods in the late Joseon Dynasty (1800s). It is currently housed in Gyujanggak, Seoul National University.

Formal Speech vs. Casual Speech

Another thing that changes depending on a social hierarchy based on age, as well as social status (i.e., ranking), is how they speak to each other. Simply put, to someone older or higher in rank than you, you need to use formal speech, while the opposite, causal speech, is used to someone younger or lower in rank than you. The easiest way for a beginner is looking at the end of a sentence. If they end in either *~yo* 요 *~nida* ~니다 *~kka?* ~까?, they are most likely *jondaetmal* 존댓말, formal speech.

Conversely, *banmal* 반말 ("informal/casual speech) can be used when talking to someone younger, the same age as you, lower in rank, or anyone who you have developed a sense of closeness and intimacy with. You can identify these as they generally end in either *~da* 다 *~ida* 이다 *~na?* 나?. The way the stories are told in this book is mainly formal for narration and a combination of both formal and casual for dialogues. We tried to show you as many variations as we could throughout the book, so you can see how they are played out in real-life situations.

Preferring Titles To Names

Along with *jondaetmal* and *banmal*, using appellations instead of names in public space (e.g., workplace) or on formal occasions (e.g., a conference) is another way Koreans used to maintain social hierarchies in the spoken language. In Korea, it is inappropriate or even rude to call someone by name. But of course, it's fine between friends and parents to children (not the other way around, though).

For example, a suffix *daek* 댁 is used to indicate a married woman who comes from that region (e.g., Busan *daek* 부산댁 meaning a married woman who comes from Busan). Also, although not related at all, people call each other using familial terms like *hyung* 형 (older brother), *nuna* 누나 (older sister), *samchon* 삼촌 (uncle), *imo* 이모 (aunt).

This makes non-Koreans wonder if all Koreans are related to each other! It's just a way Koreans show affection and get along with each other. Below is a handy table of some of the most common Korean appellations you will hear in Korean dramas.

How to Use This Book

<u>Download and Listen to Audio Files</u>
Each story has a downloadable MP3 file recorded by a professional Korean voice actor to help you learn the correct pronunciation. To maximize your learning experience, we made two versions.

- Normal Speed - Learn how Korean people would speak in normal situations.
- Slow Speed - Learn how each word and expression is pronounced.

<u>Parallel Text</u>
A parallel text, a text placed alongside its translation, is one of the most effective methods available to learn a new language, thanks to numerous advantages. This is why numerous classic works around the globe have been translated in this way. Among many advantages, it draws learners' attention to:

- Linguistic as well as cultural differences.
- Meaning, structure, and vocabulary-related aspects.
- Find similarities and differences found in literary devices such as idioms and metaphors.

And it's an optimal choice for self-study students because they can find meanings in the text and read them in context, eliminating the need to depend on a teacher. This book, optimized for beginners, will help you to obtain a thorough understanding of the Korean language.

<u>Culture Note</u>
Learn how the stories came into existence by understanding the cultural and historical aspects, so you can fully appreciate the stories, including their hidden meanings and nuances.

<u>Reading Comprehension</u>
Test and develop your Korean reading comprehension skills with quiz questions on the stories.

<u>Vocab & Proverbs</u>
Learn the essential Korean words used in the stories and related proverbs.

<u>Appendix</u>
If you're a complete beginner or just want to have a quick refresher, start here!
- How to read and pronounce the Korean alphabet
- Structure of Korean syllables and sentences
- Frequently used Korean expressions and Korean honorifics

A word on romanization: There's no romanization provided in the book because it's not an effective tool for learning the accurate pronunciation of the spoken language, as the Roman alphabet (no other alphabet can, except the Korean alphabet, for that matter) can't transcribe the Korean pronunciation. Instead, learn the accurate pronunciation of spoken Korean with our audio files and the Korean alphabet.

나무꾼과 호랑이 형님
The Woodcutter and the Tiger Brother

옛날 한 나무꾼이 산을 지나다가 호랑이를 만났습니다. 겁이 난 나무꾼은 위기를 피하기 위해 호랑이에게 말했습니다.

"아이고 형님! 우리 어머니께서 말씀하시길 저에게 형이 하나 있는데 죽어서 호랑이가 되었다고 하더니 바로 그 형님이시군요! 우리 어머님이 형님을 그리워하니 당장 뵈러 갑시다!" 라고 말했습니다.

호랑이가 그 말을 믿고서,

"지금 당장 우리 어머니를 뵙고 싶지만, 호랑이의 모습으로 그럴 수 없다"라고 거절했습니다.

자신이 사람이라고 믿었던 호랑이가 그때부터 꼬박꼬박 집 앞마당에 돼지를 가져다 놓았어요.

Once upon a time, a woodcutter met a tiger while passing through the mountain. To avoid the crisis, the scared woodcutter told the tiger,

"Oh, my brother!" Our mother told me that I have an older brother who died and became a tiger, and that's you! Our mother misses you, so let's go see her right away!"

The tiger believed that and rejected it saying,

"I want to see our mother right now, but I can't do that in the form of a tiger."

The tiger, who believed he was a human, started bringing pigs to the front yard of the house.

그 덕분에 나무꾼과 어머니는
부자로 살게 되었습니다.

몇 년 뒤 어머니께서 돌아가시자 호랑이가
돼지를 가져다 놓는 일도 멈췄습니다.

궁금해진 나무꾼이 호랑이가 살던 굴에 가 보
니 새끼 호랑이들이 있었습니다.
새끼들에게 이유를 물으니,

"우리 할머니는 인간인데 할머니께서
돌아가셨어요. 그리고 아버지도 슬퍼서 밥을
먹지 않아서 돌아가셨어요"라고 말했습니다.

나무꾼은 호랑이의 효성에 감동해서 어머니
묘옆에 호랑이의 묘를 만들어 주었습니다.

Thanks to that, the woodcutter and mother
could live as rich people.

A few years later, when the mother passed
away, the tiger stopped bringing pigs.

The curious woodcutter went to the cave
where the tiger lived and found baby tigers.
When asked the baby tigers why,

They said, "Our grandmother was a human,
but she passed away. And our father also died
as he stopped eating because he was sad."
The baby tigers responded.

The woodcutter was moved by the tiger's
filial piety and made a tomb for the tiger next
to his mother's tomb.

Culture Note

In the past, many tigers lived in Korea because of the geographical characteristics, where mountains account for 70% of the land. So, while walking along the mountain path, people often encountered tigers, and tigers looking for food often came down to where people lived and hurt people. However, Koreans also strongly perceived tigers as mystical creatures, not ordinary animals. So tigers were objects of fear, but on the contrary, they were also objects of respect. In this story, the woodcutter escapes a dangerous situation with wisdom. The image of a tiger who firmly believes that it is a person and being filial to its human mother contains the concept of filial piety that Koreans consider the most important

Vocabulary

옛날 the old days/times. **한** a, some. **나무꾼** a woodcutter. **나무** means "wood/tree" and **꾼** refers to someone who does something as a job. E.g., **사기꾼** = "con artist" because **사기** means "con/deception".

지나다 to pass-by. **지나가다** while passing by. **호랑이** a tiger.

겁이 나다 to be scared. **겁이 난** scared (adj.) **위기** a crisis.

피하기 위해 in order to avoid. **아이고** oh, my! **형님** honorific form of "older brother". **우리** we/us/our. **어머니** a mother. **말씀** honorific form of "saying".

말 "saying", but a homonym for "horse". **당장** right away.

그리워하니 because [subject] misses [object]. **그리워하다** to miss [object].

지금 now. **모습** a shape/form. **거절하다** to reject. **자신** self.

사람 / 인간 a human. **집** a house/home. **앞마당** a front yard (**앞** means "front" and **마당** means "yard"). **돼지** a pig. **덕분에** thanks to.

부자 the rich. a rich person. **멈추다** to stop. **새끼** a baby, an offspring.

이유 a reason. **할머니** a grandmother. **밥** rice/meal. **효성** filial love.

감동하다 to be moved/touched. **묘** a grave. **만들어주다** to make [object] for [subject]

Proverb

호랑이에게 물려가도 정신만 차리면 산다.
(Literal) Even if you get bitten by a tiger,
you can survive if you keep your head on straight.
No matter how hopeless it seems, you can overcome it
if you don't give up and show your wisdom.

Reading Comprehension Quiz

How did the woodcutter feel when he first encountered the tiger?
A. Happy B. Sad C. Scared D. Angry

According to the woodcutter, his older brother became a tiger after...
A. Birth B. Death C. 18th Birthday D. Marriage

The tiger started bringing pigs to the woodcutter's house to...
A. Show filial piety as a son. B. Fend off humans from entering its habitat.
C. Make fun of them. C. Teach them how to hunt pigs.

The tiger stopped bringing pigs to the woodcutter's house _______ the human grandmother's death.
A. A few months later. B. A few days before. C. During D. A few years later.

According to the story, the baby tigers didn't seem to believe that their grandmother was a human.
A. True B. False

Upon the human mother's passing, the tiger stopped eating to express...
A. Satisfaction B. Sorrow C. Ambition D. Joy

From the story, we can assume that the woodcutter felt _______ towards the tiger.
A. Thankful B. Jealous C. Angry D. Puzzled

Answer : C / B / A / D / B / B / A / B

무엇이든 거꾸로 했던 청개구리
The Green Frog That Did Everything the Other Way Around

옛날 옛적, 어느 작은 연못에 엄마 청개구리와 아들 청개구리가 살고 있었습니다.

Once upon a time, a mother green frog and a son green frog lived in a small pond.

아들 청개구리는 엄마 청개구리의 말을 듣지 않고 무엇이든 반대로 했습니다.

The son green frog did not listen to his mother and did everything opposite to what she said.

엄마 청개구리가,

If the mother green frog said,

"숲속에는 뱀이 많아 위험하니 가지 말아라"고 하면,

"Do not to go into the forest because there are many snakes",

아들 청개구리는 일부러 숲에 놀러 갔습니다.

Then the son green frog went to the forest to play on purpose.

아들 청개구리 때문에 엄마 청개구리는 매일 걱정을 했습니다.

The mother green frog was worried every day because of her son.

엄마 청개구리는 결국 병이 나서 쓰러졌습니다.

The mother green frog eventually fell ill and collapsed.

죽음이 다가온 것을 알게 된 엄마 청개구리는 아들 청개구리에게 말했습니다.

Knowing that death was approaching, the mother green frog said to her son.

“아들아, 나는 이제 얼마 살지 못할 것 같구나.
내가 죽으면 꼭 냇가에 묻어다오.”

사실, 엄마 청개구리는
산에 묻히기를 원했습니다.

하지만 이렇게 말을 해야, 아들 청개구리가
반대로 산에 묻어주리라 생각했던 것입니다.

엄마 청개구리가 죽자,
아들 청개구리는 매우 슬펐습니다.

그리고, 자신의 잘못을 뉘우치며
엄마 청개구리의 마음을 이해했습니다.

'내가 엄마 말을 듣지 않아서
엄마가 돌아가신 거야.'

아들 청개구리는 후회했습니다.
하지만 이미 엄마는 하늘나라로 떠났습니다.

아들 청개구리는,
엄마의 마지막 소원을 들어주기로 했습니다.

그래서 엄마 청개구리를
냇가에 묻어 주었습니다.

하지만 비가 오면 엄마의 무덤이
냇물에 떠내려가지 않을까 걱정했습니다.

그래서 청개구리들은 비가 오면
항상 큰 소리로 우는 것입니다.

"Son, I don't think I will live long now.
If I die, make sure to bury me near the
stream."

In fact, the mother green frog wanted to be
buried in the mountain.

But she thought that only when she said
this, the son green frog would bury her in
the mountain, doing the opposite.

When the mother green frog died, the son
green frog was very sad.

And, regretting his fault, he understood
how the mother green frog felt.

*My mother died
because I didn't listen to what she said.*

The son green frog regretted it,
but his mother had already left for heaven.

The son green frog decided to grant his
mother's last wish.

So he buried the mother green frog
near the stream.

However, he was worried that his mother's
grave would be washed away in the stream
if it rained.

That's why green frogs cry loudly
when it rains.

Culture Note

This story is a folk tale that teaches us the importance of filial piety. It provides a fun way to learn about the ecology of the tree frogs and the Korean people's efforts to interpret natural phenomena when science was not developed.

Vocabulary

어느 a (as an indefinite article). 연못 a pond. 아들 a son.

반대로 the other way. 숲 a forest. the woods. 속 inside. 뱀 a snake.

위험 a danger. 위험하니 because it's dangerous. 일부러 intentionally/on purpose. 놀러 가다 go to play. 매일 everyday. 결국 eventually.

쓰러지다 to collapse. 죽음 death. 다가오다 to come near.

냇가 the side of a stream. 꼭 surely. 산 a mountain. 원하다 to want.

잘못 a fault. 뉘우치다 to repent/to feel sorry for. 마음 mind/heart.

이해하다 to understand. 돌아가시다 to pass away/decease.

후회하다 to regret. 이미 already. 떠나다 to leave. 소원 a wish. 비 rain.

Proverb

소 잃고 외양간 고친다.
(Literal) Fix the barn after losing the cow.
Crying over spilled milk.
This is a sarcastic remark that it is useless to regret something
after things have already gone wrong.

Reading Comprehension Quiz

According to the story, we can assume that the son green frog always held a grudge against his mom.

A. True B. False

According to the story, the son green frog does not seem to be afraid of snakes.

A. True B. False

Which of the following is the most likely reason the mom green frog was worried about her son?

A. He might study too hard. B. He might help other green frogs in need.
C. He might put himself in dangerous situations.
D. He might understand the meaning of life.

According to the story, the mom green frog assumed that her son would do exactly what she asked him to do after she died.

A. True B. False

The son green frog was sad because…

A. His mom asked him to do something impossible to do on his own.
B. His mom left him no money to live on. C. It will rain every day if she died.
D. He understood how his mom must have felt.

Did the son regret his mistakes?

A. Yes B. No C. Can't tell from the story.

The mom green frog actually wanted to be buried near the stream.

A. True B. False

Answer : B / A / C / B / D / A / B

꾀 많은 토끼와 호랑이
The Cunning Rabbit and The Tiger

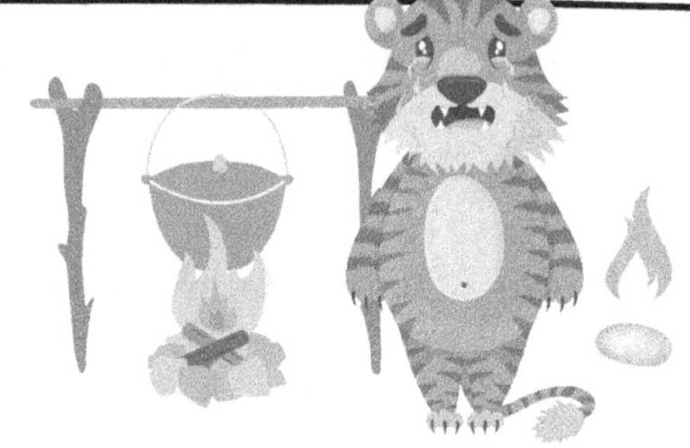

어느 날, 깊은 산 속 오솔길에서
토끼와 호랑이가 마주쳤습니다.

One day, a rabbit and a tiger met on
a deep mountain trail.

"어흥! 배가 고프니 너를 잡아 먹어야겠다."

"Growl! I'm hungry, so I'll eat you up."

호랑이가 으르렁거리며
토끼를 잡아먹으려고 했습니다.
하지만 영리한 토끼는 좋은 꾀가 떠올랐습니다.

The tiger growled and tried to eat the rabbit.
But the clever rabbit came up with a good
ploy.

"호랑이님, 떡을 구워 드릴까요?"

"Sir tiger, do you want me to grill
rice cakes for you?"

떡을 좋아하는 호랑이는 침을 흘리며 고개를 끄
덕였습니다. 토끼는 불을 피우고 돌멩이
열 한 개를 주워왔습니다.

The tiger, who liked rice cakes, drooled and
nodded. The rabbit made a fire and picked up
eleven stones.

그리고, 떡과 함께 먹을 김칫국을
가져오겠다고 말했습니다.

And it said it would bring kimchi soup to eat
with the rice cakes.

"호랑이님, 떡을 굽고 있으세요.
제가 김칫국을 가져오는 동안 떡이 익을 거예요.
하지만 떡은 딱 열 개니까 먼저 먹으면 안 돼요."

"Sir tiger, please grill the rice cakes.
The rice cake will cook while I bring my
kimchi soup. But there are only ten rice
cakes, so you shouldn't eat them first."

토끼는 재빨리 사라졌습니다.

호랑이는 기다리다 지쳐,
떡의 개수를 세어보았습니다.
열 개인 줄 알았던 떡은
열 한 개였답니다.

배가 고팠던 호랑이는 몰래
떡 하나를 먹기로 했습니다.

구워지고 있는 떡 중
가장 큰 떡을 하나 집어
얼른 입에 집어넣었지요.

"으악! 뜨거워!"

불에 잘 달구어진 돌멩이는
호랑이의 배 속을 고통스럽게 만들었습니다.
하지만 이미 토끼는 멀리 도망친 후였습니다.

The rabbit quickly disappeared.

The tiger got tired of waiting, so it counted
the number of rice cakes. There were
eleven rice cakes while the tiger thought
there were ten.

The hungry tiger decided to secretly
eat a rice cake.

It picked up one of the largest
rice cakes being grilled and quickly
put it in its mouth.

"Argh! It's hot!"

The well-heated stone made the tiger's
stomach hurt painfully, but it was already
after the rabbit ran far away.

Culture Note

Like the story of David and Goliath in the Bible, the story's moral is that, no matter how weak you are, you can overcome troubles if you demonstrate wisdom even in dangerous situations. At the same time, it warns that no matter how strong you are, you can be defeated if you look down on the other person.

Vocabulary

오솔길 a path/trail. **토끼** a rabbit. **마주치다** to run into/bump into. **잡아먹다** to prey on/to hunt and eat. **영리한** clever. **꾀** a ploy/trick. **떠오르다** to come up/float. **떡** rice cake. **침** spit/saliva. **고개** the head/a hill. **끄덕이다** to nod. **불** fire. **돌멩이** a stone/pebble. **열** ten **열한 개** eleven of (something), where **개** is the counter word to indicate the quantity of something. **먼저** first/before. **재빨리** quickly. **사라지다** to disappear. **기다리다** to wait. **지치다** to be tired/exhausted. **개수** quantity. **세어보다** to count. **배가 고프다** is hungry. **몰래** secretly. **얼른** quickly/promptly. **집어넣다** to put in. **고통** pain.

Proverb

욕심 많은 놈이 참외 제쳐놓고 호박 고른다
(Literal) The greedy one will put aside the pear and choose the pumpkin.
Excessive greed will make you go blind and lead to loss.
*The pear is perceived as more valuable than the pumpkin in this expression.

Reading Comprehension Quiz

According to the story, the rabbit was looking forward to meeting the tiger.

A. True B. False

The tiger wanted to eat the rabbit because it was…

A. Blind B. Mute C. Hungry D. Bored

The rabbit offered to grill rice cakes for the tiger out of respect.

A. True B. False

The rabbit enjoys eating cooked stones.

A. True B. False

The tiger was angry to learn that there was actually eleven rice cakes when he was told only ten.

A. True B. False

The tiger thought that even if he ate one of the rice cakes, the rabbit wouldn't notice it.

A. True B. False

The tiger was in pain because the rice cake wasn't fully cooked.

A. True B. False

Answer : B / C / B / B / B / A / B

낚시하는 호랑이
The Fishing Tiger

어느 추운 겨울날,
여우와 호랑이가 강가에서 마주쳤습니다.
호랑이는 앞발로 여우의 목을 세게 누르며
외쳤습니다.

"너는 나의 저녁 식사다!"

하지만 영리한 여우가 말했습니다.

"저에게 자비를 베푸시면, 싱싱한 물고기
잡는 법을 가르쳐 드리겠습니다."

물고기를 좋아하는 호랑이는 여우를
살려주었습니다.

여우는 호랑이를 강가 한가운데로
데려갔습니다.

그리고 얼음 구멍 속에 호랑이의 꼬리를
담그라고 했습니다.

"이렇게 꼬리를 담그고 있으면 물고기들이
와서 꼬리에 달라 붙을 것입니다."
라고 말했습니다.

호랑이는 물고기를 먹는 상상에 들떴습니다.

One cold winter day, a fox and a tiger
bumped into each other by the river.
The tiger shouted, pressing hard on the fox's
neck with its front feet.

"You're my dinner!"

But the clever fox said,

"If you show me mercy, I'll teach you
how to catch fresh fish."

The tiger, who liked fish,
let go of the fox.

The fox took the tiger to the
middle of the river.

And it told the tiger to dip its tail
in the ice hole.

"If you dip your tail like this, the fish will
come and stick to your tail," it said.

The tiger was excited at the thought of
eating fish.

하지만 시간이 지나자 점점 몸이
차가워졌습니다.

But as time passed, its body gradually
cooled down.

호랑이는 꼬리에 잔뜩 매달려 있는 물고기를
상상하며 참았습니다.

The tiger endured, imagining fish hanging
from its tail.

바로 그때, 갑자기 여우가 일어나서
집에 가겠다며 작별 인사를 건넸습니다.

Just then, the fox suddenly woke up and
bid farewell, saying it would go home.

호랑이가 여우에게 어디에 가느냐고 물었고,
토끼가 대답했습니다.

The tiger asked the fox where it was going,
and the rabbit answered,

“멍청한 호랑이가 꼬리를 빼내기 전에
서둘러 도망가야지요.”

"I'd have to quickly run away before the
stupid tiger pulls out its tail.”

호랑이는 그제야 자신이 속아버린 것을
깨달았습니다.

Only then did the tiger realize that it had
been deceived.

하지만 호랑이는 전혀 움직일 수 없었습니다.

But the tiger couldn't move at all.

호랑이의 꼬리는 이미 얼음 구멍 속에서
얼어버렸기 때문입니다.

It's because the tiger's tail has already
frozen in the ice hole.

호랑이는 멀리 사라지는 여우의 뒷모습을
바라볼 수밖에 없었습니다.

The tiger had no choice but to stare at the
back of the fox disappearing far away.

Culture Note

Foxes, along with rabbits, are animals that Koreans think are very cunning. The moral of the story is that you can overcome a difficult situation with your wisdom, and if you become too greedy, wanting more than what you already have, like the tiger, you will end up losing what you already have.

Vocabulary

추운 cold. **겨울** winter. **여우** a fox. **앞발** a front paw. *앞 means "front".

외치다 to cry out/shout. **저녁 식사** dinner meal. **자비** mercy. **싱싱한** fresh.

물고기 fish. **한가운데** in the very middle/center. **얼음** ice. **구멍** a hole.

꼬리 a tail. **담그다** to soak/immerse. **상상** imagination. **들뜨다** to be excited.

시간 time. **작별 인사** a farewell. **어디에** (to) where.

대답하다 to answer/respond. **멍청한** stupid. **전에** before/previously.

서둘러 quickly. **전혀** at all. **이미** already. **때문이다** is because -.

Proverb

바다는 메워도 사람의 욕심은 못 채운다
(Literal) You can fill the ocean, but you can't fill people's greed.
It means that people's greed is limitless.

Reading Comprehension Quiz

According to the story, the tiger didn't have dinner when it met the fox.

A. True B. False

According to the story, the river had an area that was still unfrozen.

A. True B. False

According to the story, we can say for sure that the fox also catches fish with its tail.

A. True B. False

The tiger could bear the pain from the ice-cold water because it was thrilled at the thought of…

A. Eating fish. B. Cooking fish. C. Eating both fish and the fox.

The fox thought the tiger was…

A. Brave B. Scary C. Stupid D. Smart

The tiger must have wished that he…

A. Had a longer tail. B. Knew what the fox was up to.
C. Wasn't too scary. D. Could run faster.

From the story, we can say that the fox's biggest strength is his…

A. Teeth B. Speed C. Sense of humor D. Wisdom

Answer : A / A / B / A / C / B / D

하늘이 더 잘 안다
Heaven Knows Better

아주 오랜 옛날, 시골에 한 늙은 농부가
살고 있었습니다.

A long time ago, an old farmer
lived in the countryside.

그는 수박을 재배하고 있었습니다.
그해에는 비가 많이 내리지 않았습니다.

He was growing watermelons.
It didn't rain much that year.

어느 가을 날, 농부는 수박을 따러 나갔어요.

One fall day, the farmer went out to pick the
watermelons.

하지만 가뭄 때문에, 예전만큼
수박이 크게 자라지 않아서 농부는
낙담했습니다.

However, because of the drought, the farmer
was disappointed that the watermelons did
not grow as big as before.

농부가 머리를 들어 보니
도토리나무가 있었습니다.

When the farmer lifted his head, there was an
acorn tree.

멀리서 보니, 나뭇가지마다
도토리가 수천 개가 달린 것만 같았습니다.

From a distance, it seemed like there were
thousands of acorns on each branch.

농부가 한숨을 내쉬며 말했습니다.

The farmer sighed and said,

'저 나무에 도토리 대신
수박이 자라면 좋을 텐데!'

*It would be nice if watermelons grow
on the tree instead of acorns!*

바로 그때, 다람쥐 한 마리가
도토리나무 위에 올라갔습니다.

Just then, a squirrel climbed
on the acorn tree.

그런데 나뭇가지가 흔들리면서
도토리 하나가 나무에서 떨어졌습니다.

However, as the branch shook,
an acorn fell from the tree.

그 도토리는 나이 많은 농부의
정수리를 때렸습니다.

The acorn hit the top of
the old farmer's head.

농부가 '아야!' 하고 소리쳤습니다.

The farmer shouted, "Ouch!"

농부는 아픈 정수리를 만지면서
생각했습니다.

The farmer thought
while touching the top of his head.

'역시 하늘은 나보다 잘 아는구나.

As expected, heaven knows better than I do.

만약 저 도토리가 아니라 그 큰 수박이었다면
내 머리는 박살이 났을 거야.'

If it was that big watermelon, not that acorn,
my head would have been smashed.

Culture Note

The moral of the story is in line with traditional Korean ideology. Appreciate the course of nature and do your best to work diligently in the circumstances you are in, rather than being greedy and discontent.

Vocabulary

시골 a countryside/rural area. 늙은 old/aged. 농부 a farmer.
수박 watermelon. 재배하다 to cultivate/grow. 해 the sun / a year.
가을 autumn. 가뭄 a drought. 낙담하다 to be discouraged. 머리 a head.
도토리 an acorn. 나무 a tree. 나뭇가지 a branch/limb. 한숨 sigh.
대신 instead. 다람쥐 a squirrel. 흔들리다 to be shaken. 나이 age.
정수리 the top of head. 때리다 to hit. 아픈 hurtful. 역시 as expected/also/too.
잘 well. 만약 if.

Proverb

남의 밥에 든 콩이 굵어 보인다
(Literal) The beans in other people's rice look bigger.
The grass is always greener on the other side of the fence.
An expression that figuratively refers to the human mind, where other people always seem to be in a better situation than you, although they may not be.

Reading Comprehension Quiz

According to the story, we can assume that watermelons can grow big even without rain.

A. True B. False

The farmer was disappointed because...

A. It didn't rain much. B. The watermelons didn't grow as big as they used to.
C. The watermelons didn't taste good as they used to.
D. He couldn't find any buyers.

From the story, we can assume that the acorns grow in the ground.

A. True B. False

According to the story, if watermelons grew on the trees, there will be...

A. More watermelons B. Fewer watermelons C. Bigger watermelons
D. Smaller watermelons

The acorn hit the top of the old farmer's head because...

A. A squirrel accidentally kicked it. B. The wind knocked it off the limb.
C. The tree was shaken. D. The old farmer prayed for it.

From the story, we can assume that the old farmer wouldn't have learned the lesson if it didn't happen.

A. True B. False

From the story, we can assume that the farmer's feeling towards heaven is...

A. Reverence B. Anger C. Hatred D. Confusion

Answer : A / B / B / A / C / A / A

코 없는 신랑과 입 큰 각시
The Husband Without a Nose and the Large-Mouthed Wife

옛날에 코 없는 신랑과
입 큰 각시가 살았습니다.

Once upon a time, there lived a noseless husband
and a large-mouthed wife.

어느 날, 이웃 마을에 사는 친구가
생일잔치를 한다고 편지를 보내왔습니다.

One day, a friend living in a neighboring village
sent a letter saying that he was having a birthday
feast.

코 없는 신랑과 입 큰 각시는 걱정이
태산이었습니다. 잔치에 가면,
사람들에게 놀림감이 될 것 같았습니다.

The noseless husband and the large-mouthed wife
were very worried. They thought they would be
teased by people if they went to the party.

"옳지, 여보. 좋은 생각이 났어요. "

"That's right, honey. I have a good idea."

입 큰 각시가 코 없는 신랑에게 웃으며
말했습니다. 코 없는 신랑은 궁금해하며
그것이 무엇이냐 물었습니다.

The large-mouthed wife smiled and said to the
noseless husband. The noseless husband was
curious and asked what it was.

"당신 코는 양초를 녹여서 만들고, 제 입에는
밀가루 반죽을 붙이고 그 위에 화장을 하면
아무도 모를 거예요."

"If we make your nose by melting candles,
and put flour dough on my mouth
and put makeup on it, no one will know."

부부는 기뻐하며 얼굴에 치장을
시작했습니다. 그리고 무사히
친구 생일잔치에 갈 수 있었습니다.

The couple began to decorate their faces
with joy. And they were able to go to their
friend's birthday feast without any trouble.

부부는 잔치에서 맛있는 음식들을
먹기 시작했습니다.

The couple began to eat
delicious food at the feast.

하지만 뜨거운 음식 때문에
신랑 코에 붙어 있던 양초 코가
녹아내리기 시작했습니다.
그것을 본 각시도 너무 크게 웃다가
입가에 붙은 밀가루 반죽이 떨어졌습니다.

However, the candle nose attached to the
husband's nose began to melt because of
the hot food. The wife who saw it laughed
so loudly that the dough on the side of her
mouth fell off.

그 광경을 본 사람들은 모두 웃었습니다.

Everyone who saw the scene laughed.

결국 부부는 창피한 나머지
집으로 돌아오고 말았습니다.

Eventually, the couple returned home
out of embarrassment.

“우리, 이제부터는 그냥 생긴 대로 삽시다.”

"Let's just live as we look from now on."

그리고 그 후 입 큰 각시와 코 없는 신랑은
못생긴 걸 원망하지 않았습니다.

And after that, the wife with a large mouth
and the noseless husband were not
embarrassed about being ugly.

Culture Note

The moral of the story is that you can live a happy life if you think positively even about your shortcomings. It also has the traditional Korean ideology of filial piety, which dictates that our body is a precious gift from our parents.

Vocabulary

코 a nose/snot. 신랑 a groom. 입 a mouth. 각시 a bride. 이웃 a neighbor. 마을 a village. 친구 a friend. 생일 birthday. 잔치 a party/feast. 편지 a letter. 걱정 a worry/concern. 태산 big mountain, but colloquially used to mean "huge". 놀림감 an object of mockery. 여보 honey/darling (usually between a wife and a husband). 양초 a candle. 밀가루 flour. 반죽 a dough. 화장 make-up. 아무도 no one/nobody. 부부 husband and wife. 기뻐하다 to be glad/happy. 치장 grooming/decoration. 무사히 safely. 맛있는 delicious. 음식 food/meal. 뜨거운 hot. 녹아내리다 to melt down. 떨어지다 to fall off/to drip. 광경 a scene/sight. 창피한 shameful. 그냥 just. 원망하다 to blame.

Proverb

뚝배기보다 장맛이 좋다.
**(Literal) The taste of soybean paste is
better than the (looks of the) earthen bowl it comes in.**
Appearances are often deceptive. / You can't tell a book by its cover.

Reading Comprehension Quiz

According to the story, we know why the husband doesn't have a nose.

A. True B. False

How did they receive an invitation to a birthday party?

A. Messenger B. Telepathy C. Letter D. Newspaper

Upon receiving an invitation, the couple felt…

A. Humiliated B. Angry C. Hungry D. Worried

The large-mouthed wife smiled because…

A. She thought up a good idea. B. She didn't have to go to the party.
C. She could buy new shoes. D. The friend's house was just nearby.

Based on the story, the couple thought the plan would work.

A. True B. False

Based on the story, it seems like the people at the party didn't notice their makeup at first.

A. True B. False

What caused the husband's nose to melt down?

A. Cold Weather B. Hot Weather C. Strong Wind D. Hot Food

Answer :B / C / D / A / A / A / D

은혜를 갚은 까치
The Magpie That Paid Back Kindness

옛날 한 선비가 한양에 가기 위해
산을 지나고 있었습니다.

Once upon a time, a scholar was passing
through a mountain to go to Hanyang.

그는 산에서 구렁이가 새끼 까치를
잡아먹으려는 것을 보았습니다.
선비는 새끼 까치를 구해주기 위해서
구렁이를 죽였습니다.

He saw a python trying to eat a baby magpie in
the mountain. The scholar killed the python to
save the baby magpie.

시간이 흘러 밤이 되었습니다.
선비는 잠을 잘 곳을 찾다가 집을
발견했습니다. 선비가 집에 도착하자,
아름다운 여인이 나와서 반겼습니다.
여인은 선비가 하룻밤을 머물 수 있도록
허락해 주었습니다.

Time passed and night came.
The scholar found a house while looking for a
place to sleep. When the scholar arrived at the
house, a beautiful woman came out and
welcomed him. The woman allowed the
scholar to stay overnight.

한밤중, 잠을 자던 선비는 갑자기
숨을 쉴 수 없었습니다. 선비가 눈을 떠보니
커다란 구렁이 한 마리가 선비의 목을
단단히 조르고 있었습니다.

In the middle of the night, the sleeping scholar
suddenly couldn't breathe.
When the scholar opened his eyes, a large
python was firmly strangling the scholar's
neck.

그렇습니다. 이 구렁이는 아까 낮에
선비가 죽인 구렁이의 아내였습니다.

That's right. This python was the wife of the
python that the scholar killed earlier in the day.

선비는 구렁이에게 자비를 베풀어 달라고
했습니다. 하지만 구렁이는 남편의 복수를
해야 한다고 말했습니다.

The scholar asked the python to show mercy.
But the python said it had to avenge the
husband.

대신, 구렁이는 날이 새기 전에 절에서
종이 세 번 울리면 선비를 풀어주겠다고
약속했습니다.

종을 세 번 울릴 방법이 없는 선비는
포기했습니다. 아침이 밝아 오자,
구렁이는 선비를 잡아먹으려고 했습니다.

바로 그때, 선비와 구렁이는 어디선가
종 치는 소리를 들었습니다.

종이 세 번 울리자 구렁이는 선비를
살려주었습니다. 구렁이는 멀리 사라졌습니다.

간신히 살아난 선비는 누가 종을 쳤는지
궁금했습니다. 선비가 종이 있는 곳으로
가보니 그곳에 어미 까치의 사체가
있었습니다.

자세히 보니 어미 까치의 머리에
피가 있었습니다. 어미 까치가 자신의 새끼를
살려준 은혜를 갚기 위해 자신의 목숨을
희생한 것이었습니다.

선비는 은혜를 갚고 죽은 까치를
잘 묻어주었습니다.

Instead, it promised to release the scholar if
the bell rang three times at the temple before
the day broke.

The scholar, who had no way to ring the bell
three times, gave up. As the morning came,
the python tried to eat the scholar.

Just then, the scholar and the python heard a
bell ringing from somewhere.

When the bell rang three times, the python
saved the scholar. The python disappeared
far away.

The scholar, who barely survived, wondered
who rang the bell. When the scholar went to
the place where the bell was, there was a
dead body of the mother magpie.

Looking closely, there was blood on the
mother magpie's head. The mother magpie
sacrificed her life to repay the scholar's
kindness of saving its baby.

The scholar carefully buried the magpie that
repaid the kindness.

Culture Note

Vocabulary

선비 a scholar. 한양 the old capital of Korea. 구렁이 a python. 까치 a magpie. 밤 night. 아름다운 beautiful/gorgeous. 여인 lady/woman.

허락해주다 to allow/let. 한밤중 in the middle of the night.

숨을 쉬다 to breathe. 목을 조르다 to choke/strangle the neck.

낮 daytime. 복수 revenge. 절 a Buddhist temple 방법 a method/means.

살아나다 to survive/escape. 궁금해하다 to wonder. 어미 mother.

은혜 grace/kindness.

Proverb

Reading Comprehension Quiz

According to the story, the python snuck into the scholar's house to eat the baby magpie.

A. True B. False

The scholar killed the python in order to protect his wife.

A. True B. False

Based on the story, we can guess the gender of the python, which is female.

A. True B. False

The python tried to kill the scholar by…

A. Poisoning B. Chocking C. Eating D. Pushing

What is the most likely emotion the python had towards the scholar?

A. Joy B. Grudge C. Satisfaction D. Confusion

What is the most likely emotion the magpie had towards the scholar?

A. Gratitude B. Anger C. Excitement D. Disappointment

According to the story, the magpie must have hit the bell with its…

A. Beak B. Wings C. Feet D. Head

Answer :B / B / A / B / B / A / D

흥부전
The Tale of Heungbu

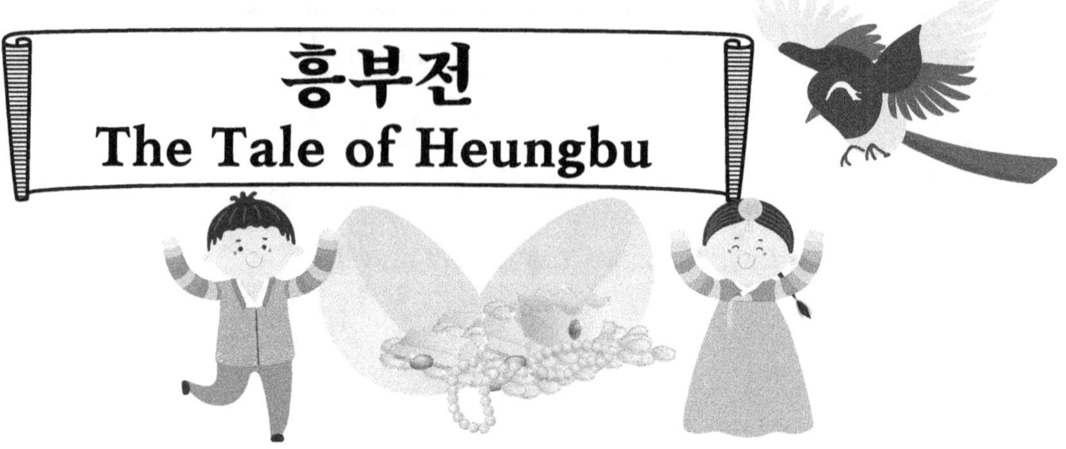

어느 날, 가난한 흥부는 형 놀부네 집에 찾아갔습니다.

One day, poor Heungbu visited his older brother Nolbu's house.

놀부는 부모님의 유산을 혼자 모두 물려받아 부자였습니다.

Nolbu inherited all of his parents' bequest by himself and was rich.

흥부는 놀부의 아내에게, 돈과 먹을 것이 없어서 그러니 한 푼만 달라고 했습니다.

Heungbu asked Nolbu's wife to give him a penny because he had no money and food.

하지만 놀부의 아내는 밥주걱으로 흥부의 뺨을 세게 쳤습니다. 그리고 흥부를 내쫓았습니다. 뺨이 퉁퉁 불은 불쌍한 흥부는 자신의 초라한 오두막으로 돌아왔습니다.

However, Nolbu's wife slapped Heungbu hard with a rice paddle, and she kicked Heungbu out. Poor Heungbu, whose cheeks were swollen, returned to his shabby cabin.

어느 봄날, 제비가 흥부네 집 마당에 떨어졌습니다. 흥부가 자세히 살펴보니 제비의 다리가 부러져 있었습니다. 흥부는 제비가 불쌍해 다리를 고쳐주었습니다.

One spring day, a swallow fell into the yard of Heungbu's house. Heungbu looked closely and found that the swallow's leg was broken. Heungbu felt sorry for the swallow, so he fixed its leg.

다음 해 봄날, 건강해진 제비가 흥부네 집에 날아왔습니다. 제비는 흥부에게 박씨를 주고 갔습니다. 흥부는 그 작은 박씨를 집 마당 한 쪽에 심었습니다.

The next spring, the swallow that became healthy again flew into Heungbu's house. The swallow gave Heungbu a gourd seed. Heungbu planted the small gourd seed on one side of the yard.

놀랍게도, 그해 가을에, 지붕이 박으로 뒤덮였습니다. 흥부와 아내는 톱을 가져와 박을 자르기 시작했습니다.

박을 열자, 귀한 보물들이 쏟아졌습니다. 그래서 흥부와 가족들은 엄청난 부자가 되었습니다.

놀부도 이 이야기를 들었습니다. 놀부가 흥부를 찾아와서, 비밀을 물어보았습니다. 착한 흥부는 놀부에게 자세히 알려주었습니다.

놀부는 곧바로 집으로 돌아왔습니다. 놀부는 제비를 잡아서, 일부러 다리를 부러뜨린 뒤 고쳐 주었습니다.

그리고 다음 해 봄, 놀부도 박씨를 받았습니다. 놀부도 박씨를 심었습니다.

그해 가을, 놀부와 아내도 톱으로 박을 열심히 자르기 시작했습니다. 놀랍게도, 박이 열리자, 무서운 괴물들이 나타났습니다.

그들은 놀부의 집을 모두 부수고 재물을 훔쳐서 사라졌습니다. 다른 박에서는 오물이 가득했습니다.

집과 재물을 모두 잃은 놀부와 아내는 슬펐습니다. 하지만 마음이 착한 흥부는 자신의 재산을 놀부와 나누었습니다.

자신의 잘못을 알게 된 놀부는 흥부에게 사과했습니다. 그 후로 형제는 행복하게 살았습니다.

Surprisingly, in the fall of that year, the roof was covered with gourds. Heungbu and his wife brought saws and began to cut the gourds.

When the gourds were opened, precious treasures poured out. So Heungbu and his family became very rich.

Nolbu also heard this story. Nolbu came to Heungbu and asked for his secret. The good Heungbu informed Nolbu in detail.

Nolbu immediately returned home. Nolbu caught a swallow, broke its leg on purpose, and fixed it.

And the next spring, Nolbu also received a gourd seed. Nolbu also planted the gourd seed.

In the fall of that year, Nolbu and his wife also began to cut the gourds with saws. Surprisingly, when the gourds opened, scary monsters appeared.

They broke all Nolbu's houses and stole his property and disappeared. The other gourds were full of filthy garbage.

Nolbu and his wife, who lost both their home and wealth, were sad. However, Heungbu, who had a good heart, shared his property with Nolbu.

Nolbu, who learned of his mistake, apologized to Heungbu. Since then, the brothers lived happily ever after.

Culture Note

The story of a greedy older brother and a foolish good younger brother is one of the most famous traditional folk tales in Korea. One of the characteristics of Korean society is that, when parents die, they bequeath all their assets only to their eldest son. This represents favoritism toward the eldest son, who can carry on the family name in the paternal-centered Korean society. In a way, this very unfair custom has led to property disputes between brothers. Many of these customs have disappeared now, but unfortunately, these problems still often occur in today's Korean society. For this reason, in traditional Korean folk tales, the older brother is often expressed as a greedy person, and the younger brother is often expressed as a poor but honest person. Through this story, you can learn about the importance of forgiveness and sharing.

Vocabulary

가난한 poor. 찾아가다 to pay a visit. 부모님 parents. 유산 heritage/bequest.

아내 a wife. 푼 penny/a Korean currency unit used in the past.

밥주걱 rice paddle. 뺨 cheeks. 초라한 shabby. 오두막 a cabin.

봄 spring. 제비 a swallow. 다리 a leg/bridge. 부러지다 to be broken.

불쌍하다 is pathetic. 고쳐주다 to repair/fix. 건강해진 became healthy.

박씨 a gourd seed. (박 means "gourd" and 씨 means "seed").

심다 to plant. 지붕 a roof. 뒤덮다 to cover. 톱 a saw. 귀한 precious.

보물 a treasure. 이야기 a story. 자세히 in detail. 부러뜨리다 to break.

열심히 hard, diligently. 무서운 scary. 괴물 a monster. 나타나다 to appear.

재물 wealth/asset. 오물 filth. 가득하다 is full of/with. 나누다 to share.

사과하다 to apologize. 행복하게 happily.

Proverb

가는 말이 고와야 오는 말이 곱다
**(Literal) If the outgoing words are beautiful,
then the incoming words will be beautiful, too.
One ill word asks another.**
It means that you have to be kind to others so that others can be kind to you.

Reading Comprehension Quiz

According to the story, Heungbu was poor because he didn't work hard.

A. True B. False

Nolbu was rich because he…

A. Stole Heungbu's money B. Found a gold mine
C. Inherited the parents' bequest D. Worked harder

How did Nolbu's wife feel when he hit Heungbu with a rice paddle?

A. Sorry B. Angry C. Grateful D. Rewarding

The swallow brought a gourd seed to express its…

A. Anger B. Grudge C. Gratitude D. Discontent

According to the story, Nolbu seems to have believed that the swallow would feel _______ towards him.

A. Grateful B. Angry C. Hostile D. Sorry

Based on the story, we can guess which of the swallow's feet was broken.

A. True B. False

Nolbu apologized to Heungbu because he…

A. Had no money. B. Regretted his faults. C. Wanted to avenge.
D. Had no other choice.

Answer :B / C / B / B / A / B / B

호랑이와 곶감
The Tiger and the Dried Persimmon

아주 옛날 어느 시골 마을에 있었던 일이에요.
배가 고픈 호랑이 한 마리가
마을로 내려왔어요.

It's a story that took place in a rural village a long time ago. A hungry tiger came down to the village.

"어훙! 저녁은 무엇을 먹을까?"

"Growl! What should I eat for dinner?"

호랑이는 입맛을 다시며 중얼거렸어요.

The tiger mumbled, smacking his lips.

바로 그때, 호랑이는 멀리서
아이가 우는 소리를 들었어요.

Just then, the tiger heard a child crying from afar.

'어떤 아이가 저렇게 울지?' 호랑이는
우는 소리를 따라서 그 집에 도착했어요.

Where is the child crying like that? The tiger followed the cry and arrived at the house.

"너 자꾸 울면 호랑이가 온다!"

"If you keep crying, a tiger will come!"

아이를 달래는 엄마의 목소리가 들렸어요.
하지만 그래도 아이는 울음을 그치지 않았어요.

The voice of the mother soothing her child was heard. But still, the child didn't stop crying.

'내가 무섭지 않은가?' 호랑이는 놀랐어요.
궁금해진 호랑이는 방문 앞에 몰래 앉았어요.
하지만 아이는 계속 울음을 그치지 않았어요.
호랑이는 더욱 궁금해졌어요.

Aren't you scared of me? The tiger was surprised. The curious tiger secretly sat in front of the door. But the child didn't stop crying. The tiger became more curious.

그때, 엄마가 말했어요.

That moment, the mom said,

"알겠다! 그래, 곶감 여기 있다!"

"Okay! Here's a dried persimmon".

그러자 아이가 울음을 뚝 그쳤어요.

Then all of a sudden the child stopped crying.

'이럴수가! 아이가 울음을 그쳤네?
곶감이 얼마나 무섭길래 아이가 저렇게
겁을 먹지?'

*Oh my! The child stopped crying! How scary
are the dried persimmons that kids get scared
like that?*

호랑이는 머릿속으로 커다란 괴물을
상상했어요. 자신보다 훨씬 무서운 괴물!
호랑이는 너무 무서워서 외양간으로
몸을 숨겼어요.

The tiger imagined a large monster in his head.
A monster that's much scarier than him! The
tiger was so scared that it hid in the barn.

그런데 얼마 후, 커다란 그림자 하나가
외양간으로 살금살금 들어왔어요.

But after a while, a large shadow crept
into the barn.

'저 녀석이 곶감인가보다!' 겁먹은 호랑이는
소 뒤에 숨었어요. 그런데 그 그림자는
호랑이의 등에 올라탔어요. 알고 보니
그 그림자는 소를 훔치러 온 도둑이었어요.

That must be the dried persimmon! The scared
tiger hid behind a cow. But the shadow got on
the tiger's back. It turned out that the shadow
was a thief who came to steal a cow.

호랑이는 곶감이라는 괴물이 자신의 등에
올라탔다고 생각했어요. 그래서 전속력으로
달리기 시작했어요.

The tiger thought that a monster called a dried
persimmon got on his back, so it started running
at full speed.

산의 중간 정도에 도착해서, 도둑은 호랑이의
등에서 떨어졌어요. 호랑이는 곶감이라고
하는 괴물이 없어졌다고 생각했어요.

Arriving in the middle of the mountain, the thief
fell from the tiger's back. The tiger thought that
a monster called a dried persimmon had
disappeared.

곶감을 무서워 한 호랑이는 두 번 다시
사람이 사는 마을에 내려가지 않았어요.

Afraid of the dried persimmons, the tiger never
went down to a human village again.

그리고, 소를 훔치려고 했던 도둑도
두 번 다시는 소를 훔치지 않았어요.

And, the thief who tried to steal a cow never
stole a cow again.

Culture Note

In the past, many tigers lived in Korea because of the geographical characteristics where mountains account for 70% of the land. So, while walking along the mountain path, people often encountered tigers, and tigers looking for food often came down to where people lived and hurt people. However, Koreans also strongly perceived tigers as mystical creatures, not ordinary animals. So tigers were objects of fear, but on the contrary, they were also objects of respect. In this story, the woodcutter escapes a dangerous situation with wisdom. The image of a tiger who firmly believes that it is a person and being filial to its human mother contains the concept of filial piety that Koreans consider the most important.

Vocabulary

마리 a counter word for animals. **내려오다** to come down. **입맛** appetite. **중얼거리다** to mumble. **아이** a kid/child. **소리** sound. **듣다** to hear/listen. **따라서** therefore. **도착하다** to arrive. **자꾸** again and again/repeatedly. **달래다** to soothe/calm. **목소리** voice. **들리다** is heard. **울음** crying. **그치다** to stop. **방문** a visit. **계속** to continue/continuance. **더욱** more. **곶감** a dried persimmon. **뚝** at once. **얼마나** how much/what degree. **머릿속** inside a head. **훨씬** way more. **외양간** a barn. **몸** a body. **숨기다** to hide. **그림자** a shade. **살금살금** silently. **등** the back. **도둑** a thief. **전속력** full speed. **중간** the middle. **정도** degree/level.

Proverb

자라 보고 놀란 가슴 솥뚜껑 보고 놀란다.
(Literal) The mind that's appalled by seeing a terrapin
is appalled by seeing a cauldron lid.
Once bitten, twice shy. / A burnt child dreads the fire.
The expression that a person who is very surprised by an object is
frightened by a similar object.

Reading Comprehension Quiz

According to the story, we can guess that tigers come down to where people live to find food.

A. True B. False

According to the story, the tiger already had dinner.

A. True B. False

The baby was crying because it was afraid of the tiger.

A. True B. False

What was the most likely reason the baby stopped crying after it was given a dried persimmon? It's what the baby…

A. Likes B. Is afraid of C. Hates D. Doesn't know

According to the story, the tiger didn't have an understanding of what a dried persimmon looked like.

A. True B. False

The thief came to steal a dried persimmon but changed his mind to steal a cow instead.

A. True B. False

According to the story, we can guess that the mom used the dried persimmon to _______ the baby.

A. Scare B. Calm C. Scold D. Understand

Answer : A / B / B / A / A / F / B

금도끼, 은도끼
The Gold Ax and the Silver Ax

옛날 한 작은 마을에 나무꾼이 살았습니다.
나무꾼은 가난했지만 착하고 정직했습니다.
나무꾼은 매일 열심히 일했습니다.

어느 날 나무꾼은 실수로
도끼를 연못에 빠뜨렸습니다.

슬프게도, 나무꾼에게는 도끼가 딱 하나밖에
없었습니다. 나무꾼은 절망해서 큰 소리로
슬프게 울었습니다.

그러자 연못에서 산신령이 나타났습니다.
그는 나무꾼에게 왜 그렇게 슬프게 우는지
물어보았습니다.

나무꾼은 산신령에게 모든 것을 설명했습니다.
산신령은 나무꾼을 불쌍하게 생각했습니다.
그래서 그를 도와주겠다고 하고 사라졌습니다.

산신령이 다시 나타났는데,
금도끼를 들고 있었습니다.

산신령은,

"이 금도끼가 네 도끼냐?" 하고 물었습니다.

Once upon a time, a woodcutter lived in a small village. The woodcutter was poor but kind-hearted and honest. The woodcutter worked hard every day.

One day, the woodcutter accidentally dropped his ax into a pond.

Sadly, the woodcutter had only one ax. The woodcutter cried sadly out loud in despair.

Then a mountain spirit appeared from the pond. He asked the woodcutter why he cried so sadly.

The woodcutter explained everything to the mountain spirit. The mountain spirit felt sorry for the woodcutter, so he said he would help him and disappeared.

The mountain spirit appeared again, but he was holding a gold ax.

The mountain spirit asked,

"Is this gold ax yours?"

나무꾼은,

"그 도끼는 제 도끼가 아닙니다."
라고 답했습니다.

산신령은 다시 사라졌습니다.
산신령이 다시 나타났는데, 은도끼를
들고 있었습니다. 그리고 그는,

"이 은도끼가 네 도끼냐?" 하고 물었습니다.

나무꾼은 이번에도 아니라고 말하며
자신의 도끼는 낡은 쇠도끼라고 말했습니다.

그러자 산신령이 다시 사라졌다가, 이번에는
금도끼, 은도끼, 쇠도끼를 모두 들고
다시 나타났습니다.

그는 나무꾼의 정직함을 칭찬 하고,
도끼 모두를 나무꾼에서 선물했습니다.

나무꾼은 산신령에게 크게 감사해하며
집으로 돌아와 행복하게 살았습니다.

한편, 옆 마을의 욕심 많은 나무꾼이 이 소문을
들었습니다. 그는 일부러 연못에 도끼를 던졌습
니다.

얼마 후 산신령이 나타나 금도끼와 은도끼를
각각 보여 주었습니다. 하지만 이 욕심 많은
나무꾼은 금도끼와 은도끼 모두 자신의
도끼라고 거짓말을 했습니다.

산신령은 화가 나서
모든 도끼를 가지고 사라졌습니다.

The woodcutter replied,

"The ax is not mine."

The mountain spirit disappeared again. The
mountain spirit reappeared, and he was
holding a silver ax. And he asked,

"Is this silver ax yours?"

The woodcutter said no again and said that
his ax was an old iron ax.

Then the mountain spirit disappeared again,
and this time, he appeared again with the
gold ax, silver ax, and iron ax.

He praised the woodcutter's honesty and
presented all the axes to the woodcutter.

The woodcutter returned home and lived
happily, greatly grateful to the mountain
spirit.

Meanwhile, a greedy woodcutter in the next
village heard this rumor. He deliberately
threw his ax into the pond.

After a while, a mountain spirit appeared and
showed a gold ax and a silver ax, respectively.
However, this greedy woodcutter lied, saying
that both the gold and silver axes were his
axes.

The mountain spirit got angry and
disappeared with all the axes.

Culture Note

Koreans have traditionally believed in shamanism. So they have believed there are divine beings not only in nature, such as mountains and seas, but also in places such as kitchens and toilets. Watching the completely different results of the woodcutter who showed honesty to the almighty mountain spirit and the woodcutter who lied, you can learn the lesson that living honestly brings good fortune while lying does the opposite.

Vocabulary

정직하다 is honest. **실수로** accidentally/by accident. **도끼** an ax.
빠뜨리다 to drop. **산신령** a mountain god. **물어보다** to ask.
설명하다 to explain. **금** gold(en). **다시** again. **은** silver. **낡은** old/worn-out.
쇠 steel/metal. **칭찬하다** to applaud. **선물하다** to gift.
감사하다 to appreciate/thank. **욕심** greed. **소문** a rumor. **거짓말** a lie.

Proverb

도둑질은 거짓말에서 시작된다.
(Literal) Stealing begins with lies.
It means if you make a habit of making small lies,
you will feel insensitive to committing a bigger crime.

Reading Comprehension Quiz

According to the story, the woodcutter was honest because he was poor.

A. True B. False

The mountain spirit appeared because...

A. It was angry that the ax polluted the pond. B. It was not a gold ax.
C. It heard the woodcutter crying. D. It wanted to scare away the woodcutter.

The most likely emotion the mountain spirit had when he appeared is...

A. Curious B. Upset C. Happy D. Tired

The most likely emotion the mountain spirit had after hearing the woodcutter's story is...

A. Compassion B. Hatred C. Anger D. Confusion

The woodcutter said the gold ax wasn't his because...

A. He wanted all three axes. B. He was honest.
C. He felt sorry for the mountain spirit. D. He was afraid of the mountain spirit.

The mountain spirit gave the woodcutter all three axes because of his...

A. Diligence B. Courage C. Honesty D. Wisdom

The most likely emotion the greedy woodcutter had after the mountain spirit took his ax is...

A. Joy B. Regret C. Harmony D. Affection

Answer :B / C / A / A / B / C / B

토끼의 간과 자라
The Rabbit's Liver and the Terrapin

옛날 옛적, 깊은 바닷속에 살던 용왕님이 심각한 병에 걸렸습니다.

Once upon a time, the Dragon King, who lived in the deep sea, got a serious illness.

신하들은 용왕님의 병을 고치기 위해 노력했지만, 효과가 없었습니다.

The servants tried to cure the dragon king's illness, but it didn't work.

바닷속에서 가장 유명한 의원이 찾아와서 용왕님의 상태를 본 후 말했습니다.

The most famous doctor in the sea came and said after seeing the Dragon King's condition.

"지상에 사는 토끼라는 동물의 간을 먹으면 나을 수 있습니다."

"You can get better if you eat the liver of an animal called a rabbit living on the ground."

용왕님의 병을 고치기 위해 충신인 자라가 지상으로 떠났습니다.

To cure the Dragon King's illness, a loyal servant terrapin left for the ground.

토끼를 본 적이 없는 자라를 위해 바닷속 화가들이 토끼의 초상화를 그려 주었습니다.

For the terrapin who had never seen a rabbit, the painters in the sea painted portraits of the rabbit.

지상에 도착한 자라는, 곧바로 토끼를 발견했습니다. 토끼를 바닷속 용궁으로 데리고 가기 위해서 자라는 꾀를 내었습니다.

Upon arriving on the ground, the terrapin immediately found a rabbit. He tried to trick the rabbit to take it to the Dragon Palace.

"바닷속 용궁은 지상보다 훨씬 살기 좋아."

"It's so much better to live in the Dragon Palace in the sea than on the ground."

자라의 말에 속은 토끼는 자라의 등에 올라타
용궁으로 떠났습니다.

용궁 신하들은 토끼를 반갑게 맞았습니다.

토끼는 기분이 좋아 어깨를 으쓱였습니다.

하지만, 용궁에 들어서자마자 토끼는
용궁 병사들에게 붙잡혔습니다.

"내 병을 위하여, 너의 간을 바치거라."

토끼는 자라에게 속은 것을 깨달았습니다.
바로 그때, 좋은 생각이 났습니다.

"용왕님을 위해서라면 저의 간을 드리겠습니다.
하지만 저의 간은 귀하기 때문에 지상의 숲속에
숨겨놓았습니다. 이것을 가져올 수 있도록
해주십시오."

이 말을 믿은 용왕은 자라와 토끼를 지상으로
보냈습니다. 지상에 도착하자 토끼는
자라의 등에서 뛰어내리며 말했습니다.

"바보 같은 녀석! 너 때문에 내가
목숨을 잃을 뻔 했다!"

그리고는 저 멀리 숲 속으로 도망쳤습니다.

The rabbit, deceived by the terrapin's
words, climbed on the terrapin's back and
left for the Dragon Palace.

The Dragon Palace officials welcomed the
rabbit. The rabbit shrugged its shoulders
in happiness.

However, as soon as it entered the palace,
the rabbit was caught by the soldiers of the
Dragon Palace.

"For my illness, offer your liver."

The rabbit realized that it had been deceived
by the terrapin. Just then, a good idea
came to mind.

"If it's for the Dragon King, I'll give you my
liver. But my liver is precious, so I hid it in
a forest on the ground. Please allow me to
bring this."

Believing this, the Dragon King sent the
terrapin and rabbit to the ground.
The rabbit, upon arriving on the ground,
said while jumping off the terrapin's back,

"You fool!
I almost lost my life because of you!"

Then it ran far away into the forest.

Culture Note

For Koreans, quick rabbits have the image of being cunning and full of tricks. On the contrary, turtles have the image of being slow and clumsy. This story's moral is that, even if you are put in a difficult situation, you can overcome it if you use wisdom.

Vocabulary

깊은 deep. 바닷속 under the sea. 용왕님 the Dragon King. 심각한 serious.

병 an illness/a disease. 걸리다 to catch. 신하 a servant/retainer/subject.

노력하다 to make efforts. 효과 effectiveness. 유명한 famous.

의원 a medical doctor. 상태 condition/state. 지상 overground.

동물 an animal. 간 a liver. 충신 a loyal servant. 자라 a terrapin.

화가 a painter. 초상화 a portrait. 곧바로 immediately.

속다 to be deceived/fooled. 반갑게 gladly. 기분 mood/feeling.

어깨 a shoulder. 으쓱이다 to shrug. 병사 a soldier. 깨닫다 to realize.

보내다 to send (away). 바보 a fool. 녀석 a guy/fellow/dude/punk. 목숨 life.

잃다 to lose. 도망치다 to escape/run.

Proverb

제 꾀에 제가 넘어간다.
(Literal) The one who sets up a ploy falls for it.
The biter gets bit.
It's an expression that means excessive deception for one's gain can lead to losses.

Reading Comprehension Quiz

According to the story, we can guess that there are no rabbits in the DragonPalace.

A. True B. False

The terrapin didn't know what a rabbit looked like, but the painters in the sea did.

A. True B. False

According to the story, the painting of the rabbit was accurate.

A. True B. False

What is the most likely reaction the terrapin had when it found the rabbit?

A. Anger B. Hunger C. Joy D. Confusion

Why did the terrapin tell the rabbit that the Dragon Palace is a better place to live?

A. To make it come to the Dragon Palace.
B. To make it scared of the Dragon Palace.
C. To warn the rabbit about the danger of the Dragon Palace.
D. To make friends with it.

According to the story, the rabbit only pretended to believe what the terrapin said.

A. True B. False

What is the most like emotion the terrapin had after the rabbit ran away?

A. Relieved B. Regretful C. Proud D. Joyful

Answer : A / A / A / C / A / B / B

거울을 처음 본 사람들
The People Who Saw a Mirror for the First Time

옛날에 시골에 사는 농부가 처음으로 한양에 가게 되었습니다.

Once upon a time, a farmer living in the countryside went to Hanyang for the first time.

농부의 부인은 남편에게 빗을 사다 달라고 부탁했습니다.

The farmer's wife asked her husband to buy a comb for her.

남편은 빗의 모양을 물었습니다. 부인은 어두운 하늘에 있는 반달을 가리켰습니다.

The husband asked about the shape of the comb. The wife pointed to the half-moon in the dark sky.

남편은 반달을 쳐다보고 고개를 끄덕였습니다.

The husband looked at the half-moon and nodded.

한양에서 며칠을 보낸 남편은, 돌아오기 전날, 부인이 부탁한 빗을 사기 위해 시장에 갔습니다.

The husband, who spent a few days in Hanyang, went to the market the day before returning home to buy the comb his wife asked.

그런데 빗의 이름을 잊어버렸습니다.

But he forgot the name of the comb.

그때, 달과 비슷한 모양이라는 부인의 말을 떠올렸습니다.

At that moment, he remembered the wife's saying that it looked similar to the moon.

그래서 하늘을 바라보았지만, 시간이 지나 달의 모양이 보름달이 되었습니다.

So he looked at the sky, but as time passed, the shape of the moon became a full moon.

그것을 본 남편은 가게주인에게
하늘의 달과 같은 모양의 물건을
달라고 했습니다.

집에 돌아온 남편은 부인에게
예쁘게 포장된 선물을 건네었습니다.
하지만 부인은 깜짝 놀랐습니다.

그 물건 안에는 부인과 옷을 똑같이 입은
젊은 여자가 있었기 때문입니다.

그것은 다름아닌 거울에 비친
자신의 모습이었습니다.

화가 난 부인은 들고 있던 것을
시어머니에게 주었습니다.

시어머니는 거울 속의 자신의 모습을 보고
되물었습니다.

"어디에 젊은 여자가 있느냐?"

After seeing it, the husband asked the store
owner to give something that looks like
the moon in the sky.

After returning home, the husband handed
his wife a beautifully wrapped gift.
But the wife was surprised.

It's because there was a young woman in
the object dressed the same as she was.

It was none other than herself in the mirror.

The angry wife gave what she was holding
to her mother-in-law.

The mother-in-law looked at herself in the
mirror and asked again,

"Where is the young woman?"

Culture Note

The two people remembered the same thing completely differently because of the changing shape of the moon. The moral of the story is that people's thoughts are all different, so their opinions may not always be the same as others'.

Vocabulary

부인 (formal) wife/missus. **빗** a comb. **남편** a husband. **부탁** a favor.
모양 a shape. **어두운** dark. **반달** crescent. **가리키다** to point at. **며칠** days.
시장 a market. **이름** a name. **비슷한** similar. **보름달** full moon. **가게** a store.
주인 a master/owner. **예쁘다** is pretty. **포장된** wrapped.
똑같이 equally/identically. **젊은** young. **여자** female/woman.
다름아닌 none other than. **비친** reflected. **시어머니** mother-in-law.

Proverb

아는 만큼 보인다.
You can see as much as you know.
It means that you should develop the ability to listen to other people's opinions,
instead of relying solely on your perspective.

Reading Comprehension Quiz

According to the story, the husband visits Hanyang often.

A. True B. False

Based on the story, the wife seems to know what combs looked like.

A. True B. False

The husband seems to have forgotten the shape of the moon his wife showed him.

A. True B. False

The husband bought a mirror instead because he couldn't afford a comb his wife wanted.

A. True B. False

The husband seems to have been aware that the mirror was actually a comb.

A. True B. False

Based on the reaction, the wife knew that the lady in the mirror was herself.

A. True B. False

Based on the reaction, the mother-in-law knew that the woman in the mirror was herself.

A. True B. False

젊어지는 샘물
The Spring Water That Makes You Younger

옛날 한 노인 부부가 있었습니다.
부부는 자식이 없어서 매일 매일 힘들게
일해야 했습니다.

Once upon a time, there was an elderly couple.
The couple had no children, so they had to work
hard every day.

어느 날 할아버지가 산에서 돌아오는 길에,
파랑새 한 마리가 날아다니는 것을
보았습니다.

One day on the way back from the mountain,
the grandfather saw a bluebird flying around.

할아버지는 그 새를 잡으려다가
깊은 산 속까지 들어갔습니다.

The grandfather went deep into the mountain
trying to catch the bird.

그곳에는 신기하게도 샘이 하나 있었습니다.

Strangely enough, there was a spring there.

마침 목이 말랐던 할아버지가
물을 세 번 마셨습니다.

Just in time, the thirsty grandfather
drank the water three times.

그리고 샘에 비친 자신의 모습을 보니,
신혼 시절의 젊은 모습으로 바뀌어 있었습니다.

And looking at himself reflected in the spring,
he was transformed into a young figure in his
honeymoon days.

밤이 깊어져 할아버지는 집에 돌아갔습니다.
그런데 할머니의 눈에는
어느 젊은 총각이 오는 것처럼 보였습니다.

As night fell, the grandfather went home. But in
grandmother's eyes, it seemed like a young
bachelor was coming.

할머니는 그 총각에게 혹시 할아버지를
보았냐고 물었습니다.

그러자 총각은 자신이 그 할아버지라고
대답했습니다. 그리고 산속에 있는 샘으로
할머니를 데리고 가서 물을 마시게 했습니다.

그러자 할머니도 새댁의 모습으로 바뀌었습니다.
둘 다 모두 신혼 시절의 모습으로
돌아가게 되었습니다.

옆집의 욕심쟁이 노인은 그 부부를 찾아가
비밀을 알게 되었습니다. 욕심쟁이 노인은
곧바로 그 샘이 있다는 산속으로 갔습니다.

그러나 욕심이 많은 노인은 물을
너무 많이 마셨습니다.

그리고 샘물에 비친 자신의 모습을 보니
갓난아기가 되어 있었습니다.

그는 샘물 옆에서 엉엉 울었지만,
그 소리는 아기의 울음소리에 불과했습니다.

The grandmother asked the bachelor if he
had seen the grandfather.

Then the bachelor replied that he was the
grandfather. And he took the grandmother
to the spring in the mountain and made her
drink the water.

Then, the grandmother changed to the
figure of a newly-maid bride. Both of them
returned to their honeymoon days.

The greedy old man next door visited the
couple and learned the secret. The greedy
old man immediately went into the
mountain where the spring was.

However, the greedy old man drank too
much water.

And when he saw himself reflected in the
spring water, he became a baby.

He bawled loudly next to the spring water,
but the sound was nothing more than a
baby's cry.

Culture Note

The "youth spring water" is certainly amazing, but too much of a good thing can be bad, like the old man who drank too much and became a baby. The moral of the story is that, if we live hard while being satisfied with what we have, good opportunities will come in the future.

Vocabulary

자식 an offspring. 파랑새 a bluebird. 할아버지 a grandfather.

신기하다 curious/extraordinary. 샘 a well/spring. 마침 just in time.

목이 마르다 is thirsty. 마시다 to drink. 신혼 honeymoon.

시절 (specific) period of time. 바뀌다 to be changed. 총각 a bachelor.

혹시 by chance/perhaps. 새댁 a newlywed bride. 옆집 the house next door.

욕심쟁이 a greedy person/ (informal) a hog. 비밀 a secret. 너무 too/so/overly.

갓난아기 a newborn baby.

Proverb

욕심이 사람 죽인다.
(Literal) Greed kills people.
It means that, if you are greedy, you cannot make rational judgments and
even do dangerous things.

Reading Comprehension Quiz

According to the story, the old couple didn't have kids because they wanted to work hard.

A. True B. False

Based on the story, the grandfather was scared of the bluebird.

A. True B. False

According to the story, it was strange that there was a spring deep in the mountain.

A. True B. False

Was the grandfather worried about drinking the spring water?

A. Yes B. No

The grandmother could instantly recognize her husband when he came back.

A. True B. False

What was the most likely emotion that the greedy old man had when he heard the story?

A. Jealous B. Peaceful C. Calm D. Relaxed

The greedy old man cried mostly likely because…

A. He was regretful. B. He was too happy. C. He was hungry. D. He wanted to sing.

Answer : B / B / A / B / B / A / A

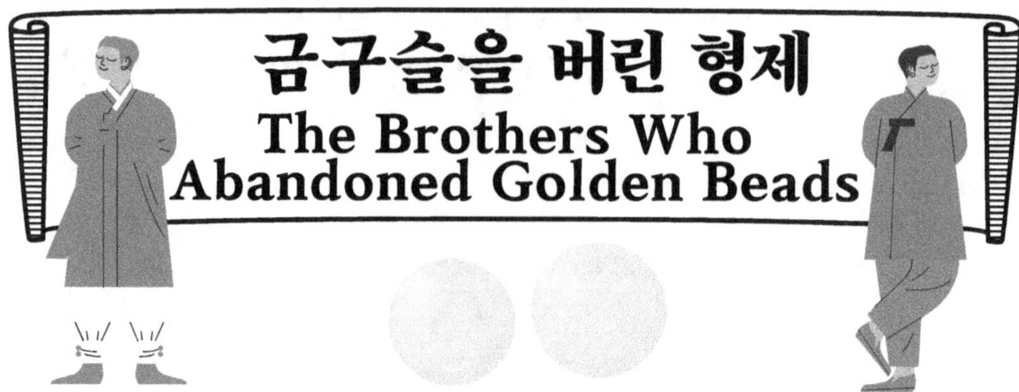

금구슬을 버린 형제
The Brothers Who Abandoned Golden Beads

옛날 어느 마을에 사이좋은 형제가 살았습니다. 형제는 기쁠때나 슬플때에 상관 없이 언제나 함께했습니다.

Once upon a time, good brothers lived in a village. The brothers were always together regardless of whether they were happy or sad.

어느 날, 형제는 강 건너 마을에 있는 잔치에 다녀왔습니다. 형제는 잔칫집에서 얻은 떡과 과일을 챙겨 집으로 돌아오고 있었습니다.

One day, the brothers went to a feast in the village across the river. The brothers were returning home with rice cakes and fruits from the feast.

집으로 돌아오는 길에, 아우는 물속에서 무언가 반짝반짝 빛나는 것을 발견했습니다.

On the way home, the younger brother found something shining in the water.

반짝반짝 빛나는 물건은 바로 금구슬이었습니다. 자세히 보니, 금구슬이 두 개나 반짝이고 있었습니다.

The shiny object was none other than a golden bead. Looking closely, he saw two golden beads shining.

형은 아우에게,

The older brother told his brother,

"너는 최근에 결혼을 했으니 돈이 필요할 것이다. 그리고 이 금구슬은 네가 먼저 발견했으니 네가 가져가거라" 말했습니다.

"You're recently married, so you'll need money. And you found these golden beads first, so you take them."

하지만 아우는 형에게,

But the younger brother told the older brother,

"식구가 많은 형님이 금구슬을 가져가세요" 라고 말했습니다.

"My brother, you have a large family, so take the golden beads."

형제는 서로에게 금구슬을 양보했습니다.
결국, 그들은 금구슬을 하나씩
나눠 갖기로 했습니다.

하지만 배가 강 한가운데를 건너갈 때쯤,

'금구슬을 준다고 할 때, 다 가질 걸 그랬군'
하고 후회했습니다.

집으로 돌아온 형제는
서로의 금구슬을 계속 생각했습니다.
그리고 형제는 자신의 금구슬을 지키느라
농사일을 게을리했습니다.

그래서 곳간은 텅텅 비기 시작했고,
가족들은 힘들어했습니다. 그제야 형제는
자신들의 잘못을 깨닫고
반성하게 되었습니다.

형은 금구슬을 들고 아우를 찾아가
금구슬을 없애야겠다고
말했습니다.

아우 역시 금구슬을 없애는 게 좋을 것 같다고
말했습니다.

형과 아우는 금구슬을 들고 다시 강 한가운데로
갔습니다.

형제는 금구슬을 꺼내 힘껏 강물에
던져 버렸습니다. 금구슬은 풍덩 소리를 내며
강 속으로 사라졌습니다.

형제는 오래오래
사이좋게 살았습니다.

The brothers yielded golden beads to each other. Eventually, they decided to share the golden beads, each taking one.

But by the time the boat crossed the middle of the river,

"I should have taken them all when he offered the golden beads." They regretted.

The brothers, who returned to their homes, kept thinking about each other's gold beads. And the brothers neglected farming to protect their golden beads.

So the shed began to empty, and the family struggled. Only then did the brothers realize their faults and reflect on themselves.

The older brother took the golden bead and visited the younger brother and said he should get rid of the golden beads.

The younger brother also said that it would be better to get rid of the golden beads .

The older brother and the younger brother took the golden beads and went back to the middle of the river.

The brothers took out the golden beads and threw them into the river with all their might. The golden beads made a splash and disappeared into the river.

The brothers lived in harmony
for a long time.

Culture Note

This story is about an ordinary family in Korea, which has traditionally been an agricultural society. Koreans made it virtuous to farm faithfully and harvest the fruits of honest efforts. Koreans considered helping each other the most important thing. So during the busy farming season, villagers took turns helping each other. Through this story, you can learn about the importance of brotherhood that money cannot buy. It also advises us to be wary of our excessive greed for wealth.

Vocabulary

사이좋은 friendly with/close to (each other). **형제** brothers.
상관 없이 regardless. **언제나** whenever. **아우** a younger brother.
반짝반짝 glittering/sparkling. **구슬** a bead/marble. **최근에** recently.
결혼 marriage. **돈** money. **필요하다** to need. **발견하다** to find out/discover.
식구 a family member. **서로에게** to each other. **양보하다** to yield.
하나씩 one by one. **농사일** farm work. **게을리하다** to slack off.
곳간 a storeroom/repository/shed. **텅텅 비다** to be completely empty.
힘들어하다 to struggle. **반성하다** to repent. **힘껏** with all one's strength.

Proverb

천석꾼에 천 가지 걱정 만석꾼에 만 가지 걱정
(Literal) A rich man with one thousand rice bags has one thousand worries,
and a rich man with ten thousand rice bags has ten thousand worries.

A metaphorical expression that means,
if you have a lot of property, you have a lot of worries.

Reading Comprehension Quiz

According to the story, the brothers didn't get along with each other.

A. True B. False

The brothers were of the same age.

A. True B. False

Based on the story, the brothers lived together.

A. True B. False

Why was the younger brother able to see the golden beads?

A. Because he was younger. B. Because he could swim.
C. Because the golden beads were shining. D. Because the golden beads were precious.

The brothers yielded the golden beads to each other because…

A. They were valuable. B. They were heavy. C. They would bring bad fortune.
D. They were scary.

The brothers were getting poorer because…

A. The golden beads were stealing their money. B. They believed the golden beads would bring them a fortune. C. They didn't work hard as they were only concerned about protecting their golden beads. D. The golden beads were actually metal beads.

According to the story, the King must have felt _________ upon hearing the story.

A. Jealous B. Furious C. Angry D. Impressed

Answer : B / B / B / C / A / C / D

용왕님의 딸, 잉어 색시
The Carp Wife – The Dragon King's Daughter

옛날 옛적, 강가에서 혼자 사는 어부가
큰 잉어를 잡았습니다. 그런데 잉어를 보자
갑자기 이런 생각이 들었습니다.

'이렇게 큰 잉어를 죽이면
분명히 벌을 받을 거야.'

그래서 집으로 돌아온 어부는
잉어를 죽이지 않고
항아리 안에 넣어 길렀습니다.

그런데, 하루는 밖에 나갔다 돌아오니
방에 밥상이 차려져 있었습니다.

'아니, 나 혼자 사는 집인데...
누가 밥상을 차려 놓았지?'
어부는 생각했습니다.

다음 날, 어부는 일하러 가는 척하다가
몰래 숨어서 집안을 들여다보았습니다.

항아리에서 잉어가 색시 모습으로
변해서 나오는 것을 보았습니다.

잉어 색시는 부엌에서 밥을 지었습니다.
그리고 다시 항아리로 들어가려고 했습니다.

Once upon a time, a fisherman living alone by
the river caught a large carp. But when he saw
the carp, this thought suddenly
came to his mind.

*If I kill such a big carp,
I will definitely be punished by heaven.*

So the fisherman who returned home
did not kill the carp but put it in a jar
and raised it.

However, one day, when he came back from
outside, dinner was prepared in the room.

*This is weird. I live alone in this house...
Who prepared dinner?* The fisherman thought.

The next day, the fisherman pretended to go to
work but hid secretly and looked into the house.

He saw the carp in a jar turning into a maiden
and coming out.

The carp maiden cooked in the kitchen.
And she tried to get back into the jar.

"색시! 잉어 색시!"
어부가 부르자 잉어 색시는 무척 놀라더니
이렇게 말했습니다.

"저는 용왕님의 딸이랍니다.
세상 구경을 하려고 나왔다가
잡혀버렸지요.
저를 살려주셔서 정말 감사해요"

"색시, 저는 혼자 사는 처지인데
저와 결혼해 주시오"
총각이 용기를 내어 말했습니다.
그러자 색시가 대답했습니다.

"하지만 조건이 있어요, 제가 목욕하는 것은
일 년 동안 절대 쳐다보지 말아 주세요."

"알겠소. 약속을 지키겠습니다."

그렇게 어부는 잉어 색시와 함께
살 게 되었습니다.

일 년이 다 되어가던 어느 날,
너무도 궁금했던 어부는 몰래
색시가 목욕하는 것을 훔쳐보았습니다.
그러자 색시는 곧 잉어로 변했습니다.

잉어가 말했습니다.

"일 년 동안 약속을 지켜주셨다면
저는 영원히 사람이 될 수 있었을 텐데…"

결국 어부는 눈물을 흘리며 잉어를
강에 놓아주었습니다.

"Lady, carp lady!"
When the fisherman called, the carp maiden
was very surprised and said this,

"I'm the daughter of the Dragon King.
I went out to see the world and
was caught.
Thank you for letting me live."

"Lady, I'm a bachelor living alone.
Please marry me."
The bachelor said with courage.
Then the carp maiden replied.

"But there's a condition. Please never
watch me take a bath for a year."

"Okay. I'll keep my promise."

That's how the fisherman ended up living
together with the carp maiden.

One day, near the end of the first year,
the fisherman, who was so curious,
secretly peeped at his wife taking a bath.
Then the wife soon turned into a carp.

The carp said,

"If you kept your promise for a year,
I could have become a human forever..."

Eventually, the fisherman shed tears
and let the carp into the river.

Culture Note

Due to the influence of traditional shamanism beliefs, Koreans consider animals such as tigers and carp to be mystic. Among the legends of the birth of ancient kings in Korea, there are stories of carp turning into a human or a child born from a large gourd. Through the sad story of the carp bride and bachelor, we can learn the importance of loyalty.

Vocabulary

혼자 alone/by oneself. 어부 a fisherman. 잉어 a carp. 갑자기 suddenly.
이런 such/like this. 분명히 clearly/obviously. 벌 punishment.
항아리 a pot/jar. 밥상 a dining table. 누가 who/whom. 다음 next.
들여다보다 to look/peep into. 색시 a maiden/lady. 나오다 to come out.
부엌 the kitchen. 무척 very/extremely.이렇게 like this. 세상 world.
구경 sightseeing. 구경꾼 a spectator. 용기 courage. 조건 a condition/term.
목욕 bath. 년 year. 동안 during. 그렇게 such/like that. 너무도 too/so/overly.
훔쳐보다 to steal a glance at/to peep at. 영원히 eternally. 눈물 tear(s).

Proverb

달면 삼키고 쓰면 뱉는다.
(Literal) Swallow what tastes sweet and spit out what tastes bitter.
It refers to a person who does something only if it is beneficial or advantageous and not keeping promises.

Reading Comprehension Quiz

According to the story, the fisherman believed the carp he caught was an extraordinary one.

A. True B. False

The fisherman put it in a jar to...

A. Cook it. B. Raise it. C. Kill it. D. Sell it.

Based on the story, we can assume that _______ usually prepares dinner.

A. His wife B. Himself C. His mother D. His younger brother

According to the story, the carp maiden was making dinner for the fisherman because she was...

A. Holding a grudge against him. B. Thankful for sparing her life.
C. Supposed to deliver an important message from the Dragon Palace.
D. Learning how to become a human.

Based on the story, we know that the Dragon King has more than one daughter.

A. Yes B. No

The bachelor didn't know that the carp was actually the Dragon King's daughter when he caught it.

A. True B. False

The carp wife turned back into a carp because her husband...

A. Didn't love her wholeheartedly. B. Wasn't being completely honest with her.
C. Didn't believe that she was the Dragon King's daughter.
D. Broke his promise.

Answer : A / B / B / B / B / A / D

요술부채
The Magic Fan

하늘나라의 옥황상제는
빨간 부채와 파란 부채를 갖고 있었습니다.

The Jade Emperor of heaven had
a red fan and a blue fan.

어느 날, 옥황상제는 부채들을
인간들이 사는 지상으로 떨어뜨렸습니다.

One day, the Jade Emperor dropped his fans to
the ground where humans live.

숲을 지나가던 나무꾼이
그 부채들을 주웠습니다.
더위에 지쳐있던 나무꾼은
그늘에 앉아 부채질하기 시작했습니다.

A woodcutter passing through the forest
picked up the fans.
The woodcutter, tired of the heat,
sat in the shade and began to fan.

나무꾼이 빨간 부채로 부채질을 하니,
코가 기다랗게 늘어났습니다.

As the woodcutter fanned himself with the red
fan, his nose stretched long.

깜짝 놀란 나무꾼은 서둘러 파란 부채로
부채질을 하기 시작했습니다.

Surprised, the woodcutter hurriedly began
fanning with the blue fan.

그러자 신기하게도 코가 조금씩 줄어들어
원래의 모습이 되었습니다.

Strangely enough, his nose gradually
decreased and became its original shape.

나무꾼은 마을 최고 부자의 집으로 향했습니다.
나무꾼은 부자에게 신기한 마법을
보여주겠다고 했습니다.

The woodcutter headed to the house of the
richest man in the village. The woodcutter said
he would show the rich man strange magic.

그리고 나무꾼은
부자의 얼굴에 빨간 부채로 부채질을 하기
시작했습니다. 부자의 코는 길게 늘어났습니다.
나무꾼은 곧바로 집으로 돌아왔습니다.

The woodcutter began fanning the rich man's
face with the red fan.
The rich man's nose stretched long.
The woodcutter immediately returned home.

코가 흉칙하게 길어진 부자는 충격을 받아
쓰러졌습니다. 유명한 의원들도 치료가
불가능하다며 포기했습니다.

부자는 자신의 병을 고쳐주는 사람에게
금화를 주겠다고 약속했습니다.
나무꾼은 그제야 파란 부채를 들고
다시 부자를 만났습니다.

"제가 병을 고쳐주면 정말로
금화를 받을 수 있지요?"

나무꾼의 질문에 부자는 그러겠다고
하였습니다. 나무꾼은 파란 부채로
부채질을 해주었습니다.
부자의 코는 다시 줄어들었고,
나무꾼은 금화를 받았습니다.

나무꾼은 어느 날, 자신의 코에 빨간 부채로
부채질을 하기 시작했습니다.
자신의 코가 얼마나 길어질지
궁금해졌기 때문입니다.

나무꾼의 코는 계속 커져서,
옥황상제님이 사는 하늘나라까지 닿았습니다.
나무꾼의 코에 걸려 넘어진 옥황상제님은
화가 났습니다. 옥황상제님은 나무꾼의 코를
기둥에 꽁꽁 묶어두었습니다.

기둥에 코가 묶인 나무꾼은 코가 아파지기
시작했습니다. 그래서 곧바로 파란 부채로
부채질을 하기 시작했습니다. 코가 줄어들며,
몸이 하늘로 떠오르기 시작했습니다.

이러한 상황을 모르는 옥황상제는 나무꾼을
용서하기로 하고, 코를 풀어주었습니다.
나무꾼은 땅으로 곤두박질쳐버렸습니다.

The rich man, whose nose became horribly
long, collapsed in shock. Famous doctors also
gave up, saying it was impossible to treat.

The rich man promised to give gold coins to
those who could heal his illness. Only then
did the woodcutter meet the rich man again
with a blue fan.

"If I cure your illness,
can I really get gold coins?"

To the woodcutter's question, the rich man
said he would. The woodcutter fanned him
with the blue fan. The rich man's nose shrunk
again, and the woodcutter received gold coins.

One day, the woodcutter began fanning his
nose with the red fan, because he wondered
how long his nose could get.

The woodcutter's nose continued to grow and
reached the heaven where the Jade Emperor
lived. The Jade Emperor, who tripped over the
woodcutter's nose, got angry.
The Jade Emperor tied the woodcutter's nose
tightly to a pillar.

The woodcutter with his nose tied to a pillar
began to feel sore. So he immediately started
fanning with the blue fan. His nose decreased,
and his body began to rise into the sky.

The Jade Emperor, who did not know this
situation, decided to forgive the woodcutter
and untied the nose. The woodcutter
plummeted to the ground.

Culture Note

In traditional Korean ideology, an omnipotent being rules the human world in heaven. The Jade Emperor is one of them. This story has the purpose of encouraging good while punishing evil and gives us the lesson that you will eventually get punished for being excessively greedy.

Vocabulary

하늘나라 sky kingdom/heaven. 옥황상제 the Jade Emperor. 빨간 red. 파란 blue. 부채 a fan. 더위 the heat. 그늘 shade. 부채질 the act of fanning. 기다랗다 is long. 늘어나다 to get extended. 조금씩 little by little. 줄어들다 to shrink. 원래 originally. 최고 the best. 마법 magic. 얼굴 the face. 흉칙하게 horribly/hideously. 충격 a shock. 불가능하다 is impossible. 금화 (a) gold coin. 약속하다 to promise. 정말로 really/truly. 질문 a question. 닿다 to reach. 걸려 넘어지다 to trip and fall. 기둥 a pillar. 묶어두다 to tie up. 상황 a situation. 용서하다 to forgive. 풀어주다 to release/let go. 곤두박질치다 to plummet.

Proverb

욕심은 끝이 없고 불평은 한이 없다
(Literal) Greed never ends and complaints know no limit.
People should learn to be satisfied with what they have or they will never be happy.

Reading Comprehension Quiz

According to the story, the Jade Emperor likes the red fan more than the blue one.

A. True B. False

According to the story, the woodcutter knew what would happen if he used the fans.

A. True B. False

Based on the woodcutter's reaction, we can assume that he always wanted to have a longer nose.

A. True B. False

The woodcutter went to the rich man's house to sell the fans.

A. True B. False

When he visited the rich man's house, the woodcutter knew what would happen if he used the fans.

A. True B. False

Based on the story, we can assume that the Jade Emperor didn't mean to take the woodcutter's life.

A. True B. False

Answer : B / B / B / B / A / A / A

깨진 유리그릇
The Broken Glass Bowl

옛날 옛적, 어느 마을에
부자 노인이 살고 있었습니다.

Once upon a time, there lived a rich old man
in a village.

노인은 빛깔이 곱고 아름다운 유리그릇이 두 개
있었습니다.

The old man had two beautiful glass bowls
with lovely and fine colors.

노인은 이 유리그릇들을 마치 자식처럼 여기며
매일 정성스럽게 닦았습니다.

The old man treated these glass bowls as if
they were children and carefully polished them
every day.

어느 날, 노인이 집을 비운 사이
하녀가 방을 청소하기 시작했습니다.
하지만 하녀는 실수로
노인이 아끼던 유리그릇 하나를 깨뜨렸습니다.

One day, while the old man was away, the
maid began to clean the room. However, the
maid accidentally broke a glass bowl that the
old man cherished.

하녀는 겁에 질렸습니다.
하녀는 소리 내어 울기 시작했습니다.
얼마 후, 하녀의 울음소리를 듣고
노인의 아내가 들어왔습니다.

The maid was engulfed in fear. The maid
began to cry out loud. A moment later, the old
man's wife came in after hearing
the maid's cry.

하녀는 바닥에 엎드려서 용서를 빌었습니다.
아내 역시, 노인이 아끼던 유리그릇이 깨진 것을
보고 깜짝 놀랐습니다. 하지만 마음씨 착한
아내는 하녀를 달래주었습니다.

The maid laid on the floor and begged for
forgiveness. The wife was also surprised to see
the broken glass bowl that the old man had
cherished. However, the kind-hearted wife
soothed the maid.

날이 어두워지자 노인이 집으로 돌아왔습니다.
그리고 유리그릇이 하나밖에 없는 것을
발견했습니다. 아내가 노인에게 말했습니다.

As it got dark, the old man returned home.
And he found that there was only one glass
bowl. The wife told the old man,

“제가 잘못해서 깨뜨렸습니다. 용서해주세요.”

"I broke it by mistake. Please forgive me."

노인은 무섭게 화를 냈습니다.
그때 하녀가 무릎을 꿇고 빌기 시작했습니다.
사실은 자신이 그랬다고 고백했습니다.

The old man became frighteningly angry. And at that moment, the maid began to kneel and beg. She confessed that it was actually her that did it.

하지만 노인은 절대로 용서할 수 없다며
소리쳤습니다.

But the old man shouted that he'd never forgive her.

바로 그때, 하녀가 일어났습니다.
그리고, 나머지 하나 남은 유리그릇을
깨뜨렸습니다. 노인은 머리끝까지 화가 나서는
하녀를 무섭게 노려보았습니다.
하녀는 흐느끼며 말했습니다.

Just then, the maid stood up. And she broke the remaining glass bowl. The old man got angry to the tip of his head and stared fiercely at the maid. The maid sobbed and said,

“저는 이미 죽은 것과 같습니다.
하지만 다른 사람이 남은 유리그릇을 깨뜨리고
죽게 될까 봐 미리 그것을 깨뜨린 것입니다.”
하녀의 말에 노인은 놀랐습니다.

"I'm already as good as dead. But I broke the remaining in advance because I was afraid someone else would break it and die."
The old man was surprised by the maid's words.

조용히 듣고 있던 아내가 말했습니다.

The wife, who was quietly listening, said,

“여보, 유리그릇을 깨뜨린 것은 잘못이지만
어찌 유리 그릇이 사람 목숨보다 귀하겠습니까?”

"Honey, it's wrong to break a glass bowl, but how can a glass bowl be more precious than human life?"

노인은 한참 동안 말이 없었습니다.
얼마 후, 노인은 미소를 지으며 말했습니다.

The old man didn't talk for a long time. After a while, the old man smiled and said,

“당신이 맞는 말을 했소.
다시는 이런 일로 화를 내지 않겠소.”

"You said the right thing. I will never get angry about things like this again."

그 후로 노인은 유리그릇들을 소중하게 여기지
않았습니다. 아무리 멋진 유리그릇이라도
사람보다 귀하지 않다는 것을 마음 깊이
깨달았기 때문입니다.

Since then, the old man has not valued glass bowls, because he realized deeply that no matter how wonderful a glass bowl is, it is not more precious than a person.

Culture Note

In traditional Korea, a paternal society, the head of the household had absolute power to take charge of all decision-making. So breaking his favorite glass bowl meant a big punishment. In this story, you can think of human dignity rather than material things. Also, you can learn the wisdom of his wife that saved the maid and enlightened her husband even in difficult situations.

Vocabulary

빛깔 color/hue. 곱다 beautiful/fine/lovely. 아름답다 is beautiful. 유리 glass. 그릇 bowl/dish. 마치 as if. 여기다 regard/consider. 정성스럽게 carefully. 사이 during/while. 하녀 a maid/(female) servant. 청소하다 to clean. 아끼다 to cherish. 겁에 질리다 to be scared/horrified. 바닥 bottom/floor. 엎드리다 to lie (with one's) face down/prostrate. 마음씨 mind/heart. 어두워지다 to get dark. 하나밖에 nothing but one. 사실은 in fact/actually. 무릎 knee. 고백하다 to confess. 나머지 remaining/a remainder. 머리끝까지 to the top of (one's) head. 노려보다 to scowl/look daggers at. 다른 사람 someone else. 조용히 quietly. 한참 동안 for a long while. 미소 a smile. 아무리 no matter how.

Proverb

말 한마디로 천냥 빛 갚는다.
(Literal) You can pay off a debt of thousand nyang with a single speech.
A good tongue is a good weapon. / A gentle word opens an iron gate.
It is an important ability to speak well, and if you speak well,
you can solve difficult or seemingly impossible things.

Reading Comprehension Quiz

According to the story, the old man had more than two glass bowls.

A. True B. False

The maid was scared because she wasn't supposed to clean the old man's room.

A. True B. False

The wife was surprised because...

A. The glass bowl was missing. B. The glass bowl was broken.
C. The glass bowl was of a different color. D. The glass bowl was heavy.

What was the most likely emotion of the old man when he returned home?

A. Frightened B. Peaceful C. Exhausted D. Hopeless

The old man got infuriated because he found out that...

A. The maid cleaned his room. B. His wife lied to him.
C. The glass bowl was broken. D. The maid actually stole the glass bowl.

The maid broke the other glass bowl to...

A. Make a point that life is more important than a glass bowl. B. Show her anger.
C. Prove her innocence. D. Prove the wife's innocence.

Based on the story, we can assume that the old man no longer cherished glass bowls because...

A. He couldn't afford them anymore. B. He thought they were fragile.
C. He learned a lesson that life is more precious.
D. He loved himself more than anything.

Answer : B / B / B / A / C / A / C

참외와 황소
The Pear and the Ox

옛날 어느 마을에 한 농부가 있었습니다.
농부는 가난했지만 부지런하고
인정도 많았습니다. 농부는 정성껏
참외 농사를 지었습니다. 여름이 되자,
노란 참외가 탐스럽게 열렸습니다.

농부는 잘 키운 참외를 마을 사람들에게
골고루 나누어 주었습니다.

그런데 그 중에서
유난히 크고 탐스러운 참외를 발견했습니다.
농부는 이 귀한 참외를 원님에게
가져가기로 했습니다.

이 마을의 원님은 어질고
지혜로웠기 때문입니다.
원님은 참외를 받고 크게 기뻐했습니다.

"이렇게 귀한 선물은 처음이구나. 여봐라,
요즘 들어온 것 중에 가장 귀한 것이 무엇이냐?

원님이 이방에게 물었고 이방은
황소 한 마리가 있다고 말했습니다.
원님은 그 황소를 농부에게 상으로 주었습니다.

착한 농부는 참외 하나로
황소를 얻을 수 있었습니다.
착한 농부가 상을 받았다는 이야기는
금방 널리 퍼졌습니다.

Once upon a time, there was a farmer in a village. The farmer was poor, but he was diligent and very compassionate. The farmer carefully grew pears. As the summer came, delicious-looking yellow pears came into bearing.

The farmer distributed the pears evenly to the villagers.

But among them, he found an exceptionally large and delicious-looking pear. The farmer decided to take this precious melon to the magistrate.

It's because the magistrate of this village was benevolent and wise. The magistrate was very happy to receive the pear.

"I've never seen a gift this precious. Hey there, what's the most precious thing that came in these days?"

The magistrate asked a government official, and he said there was an ox. The magistrate gave the farmer the ox as a prize.

The good farmer was able to get an ox with one pear. The story that a good farmer received an award quickly spread.

같은 마을에 사는 욕심쟁이는
이 소문을 듣고 온종일 배가 아팠습니다.
그리고, 자신도 똑같이 따라 하려고
마음먹었습니다.

하지만 이미 착한 농부가 가져갔던 참외를
또 가져갈 수는 없었습니다. 욕심쟁이는
당장 외양간으로 달려갔습니다.
외양간에서 병든 황소를 끌고
원님 앞으로 몰고 갔습니다.

"제가 평생 소를 키웠지만 이렇게 크고 튼튼한
황소는 처음입니다. 받아주십시오."

원님은 황소를 보고 욕심쟁이의 속내를
눈치챘습니다. 지혜로운 원님은 이방을
불렀습니다.

"여봐라, 요즘 들어온 것 중에
가장 귀한 것이 무엇이냐?"

욕심쟁이는 무슨 귀한 선물을 받을까
궁금했습니다. 황금? 보석? 하지만
이방의 대답을 듣고 깜짝 놀랐습니다.

"얼마 전에 들어온 크고 귀한 참외가 있습니다."
"잘됐구나. 그 참외를 이 사람에게
상으로 주어라."

집으로 돌아온 욕심쟁이는
울음을 터뜨렸습니다.

욕심쟁이는 괜한 욕심으로 황소를
참외와 맞바꾸게 되었답니다.

The greedy man living in the same village was
sick to his stomach with jealousy all day after
hearing this story. And, he decided to follow
the same way.

But he couldn't take another pear that the good
farmer had already taken. The greedy man
immediately ran to the barn. He dragged an
old and sick ox from the barn and dragged it in
front of the magistrate.

"I've raised cows all my life, but I've never had
an ox this big and strong. Please accept it."

When the magistrate saw the bull, he noticed
the greedy man's inner motives. The wise
magistrate called the government official.

"Hey there, what's the most precious thing that
came in these days?"

The greedy man was curious about what
precious gift he would receive. Gold?
Jewelry? But he was surprised to hear the
answer from the government official.

"There is a big and precious pear
that came in not too long ago."
"That's great. Give the pear to this person
as a prize."

After returning home, the greedy man
burst into tears.

The greedy man exchanged the ox for a pear
because of his useless greed.

Culture Note

Vocabulary

부지런하다 is diligent. 인정 많다 is compassionate. 참외 the pear.

농사를 짓다 to farm. 여름 summer. 노란 yellow.

탐스럽게 deliciously/attractively. 열리다 to ripen/to open.

골고루 evenly/equally. 그중에서 among them. 유난히 especially.

원님 a magistrate. 어질다 is benevolent. 지혜롭다 is wise.

여봐라 hey, there/hey, you. 요즘 nowadays. 이방 a government official.

황소 an ox. 상 a reward/award. 얻다 to gain/obtain.

금방 soon, quickly, any minute. 널리 widely. 퍼지다 to get spread.

온종일 all day long. 배가 아프다 (lit) stomach hurts. = is jealous.

마음먹다 to decide. 병든 ill/sick. 튼튼한 sturdy/strong.

받아주다 to accept (for someone). 속내 inner motive. 괜한 useless/pointless.

맞바꾸다 to trade/exchange.

Proverb

오르지 못할 나무는 쳐다보지도 마라.
(Literal) Don't even look at the tree you can't climb.
It means that it is better not to think about something that's beyond your ability.

Reading Comprehension Quiz

According to the story, the farmer was poor because he was compassionate.

A. True B. False

According to the story, we can guess that pears ripen during the summer season.

A. True B. False

The farmer shared the pears with the villagers because…

A. The pears went bad. B. The pears weren't valuable.
C. The farmer didn't know the value of the pears. D. The farmer was kind-hearted.

The magistrate gave an ox to the farmer as a…

A. Punishment B. Peace Offering C. Homework D. Reward

According to the story, we can assume that the greedy man believed that the magistrate wouldn't find out that it wasn't a good ox.

A. True B. False

The greedy man wasn't expecting to receive anything valuable from the magistrate.

A. True B. False

According to the story, the greedy man thought a good pear is more valuable than a sick ox.

A. True B. False

Answer : B / A / D / D / A / B / B

사이좋은 형제와 신비한 볏단
The Good Brothers and the Mysterious Rice Sheaves

옛날 아름다운 시골 마을에
우애 깊은 형제가 있었답니다.

Once upon a time in a beautiful rural village,
there were brothers with deep fraternal love.

형제는 서로를 도우며
열심히 일했습니다.

The brothers worked hard,
while helping each other.

가을이 되자 많은 곡식을 수확했습니다.
형제는 곡식을 사이좋게 똑같이 나누었습니다.

In autumn, a lot of grain was harvested. The
brothers shared the grain equally.

그날 밤, 집으로 돌아간 형은
곰곰이 생각 했습니다.

That night, the older brother, who returned
home, pondered.

'아우는 최근에 장가를 갔으니
필요한 게 많을 거야.
볏단을 좀 나누어 주어야지'

My younger brother got married recently,
so he'll need a lot of things.
I'm going to hand out some rice sheaves.

밤에 몰래 집을 나온 형은
아우 집의 곳간에 볏단을 올려놓고
기분 좋게 돌아왔습니다.

The older brother, who secretly snuck out of
the house at night, came back pleasantly after
leaving the rice sheaves in the shed of his
brother's house.

그런데 아우도 마찬가지로
이런저런 생각을 하고 있었습니다.

But the younger brother was also thinking
about many things.

'형님은 식구도 많고
부모님 제사도 모셔야 하니
볏단이 많이 필요할 거야'

My older brother has a large family and he
has to hold ancestral rites for our parents as
well, so he'll need a lot of rice sheaves.

그리고는 아우는
자기의 곳간에서
볏단을 가져와 형 집의 곳간에 몰래 놓고
흐뭇해했습니다.

다음 날 아침에 일어난 형제는 놀랐습니다.
자기 집 곳간의 볏단이
그대로였기 때문입니다.

형제는 이상하다고 생각했지만,
서로에게 이야기할 수가 없었습니다.
만약 서로가 이 사실을 알면
받지 않을 것이 뻔했기 때문이었습니다.

밤이 되자 형제는 다시 지난밤처럼
볏단을 옮겨 놓았습니다. 그러나 아침이 되면
볏단은 여전히 그대로였습니다.

'오늘은 일찍 가서
남은 볏단을 세어봐야지'

다음 날 저녁,
다시 볏단을 지고 아우 집으로 갔습니다.

그런데 저 멀리 희미한 달빛 속에서
누군가 볏단을 지고 오는 것을 보았습니다.

그림자가 점점 가까워졌을 때
형은 그 사람이 아우라는 것을 알았습니다.
동생도 달빛에 비친 사람이
형이라는 것을
알게 되었습니다.

서로를 생각하며
자신의 것을 나누어 주려던 형제는
서로를 보며 웃었답니다.

And then the younger brother took the rice
sheaves from his shed and secretly placed
them in the shed of his brother's house
and felt pleased.

The brothers who woke up the next morning
were surprised, because the rice sheaves in
their houses' sheds remained the same.

The brothers thought it was strange, but they
couldn't talk to each other, because it was
obvious that they would not accept it if they
knew this.

At night, the brothers moved the rice sheaves
again like the night before. But in the
morning, the rice shaves were still the same.

I'm going to go early and
count the remaining rice sheaves.

The next evening, the older brother took the
rice sheaves back to his brother's house.

But in the dim moonlight far away,
he saw someone bringing a rice sheave.

As the shadow got closer and closer, the older
brother knew that it was his younger brother.
The younger brother also found out that the
person reflected in the moonlight was
his older brother.

The brothers, who were trying to give out
what they had while thinking about each other,
smiled at each other.

Culture Note

In traditional Korean folk tales, the older brother is often depicted as a character with a lot of wealth but too greedy. This is because the eldest son inherits all of his parents' inheritance due to Confucianism in Korea. But in this story, the brothers show how they care for and love each other. The moral of the story is that family is more precious than wealth and that, if you help others, good fortune will find you.

Vocabulary

우애 깊은 with deep fraternal love. **돕다** to help. **곡식** grain. **수확하다** to harvest. **곰곰이** carefully/deliberately/thoroughly.

장가 a male marrying a female. The opposite is **시집**, a female marryig a male. **볏단** a rice sheave. **좀** a little. **이런저런** this and that. **제사** ancestral rite. **모시다** to serve/support. **많이** a lot/plenty. **흐뭇해하다** to feel pleased. **아침** morning. **그대로** like it/as-is. **이상하다** is strange. **뻔하다** clear/obvious/predictable. **여전히** still. **일찍** early. **남은** remaining. **희미한** dim/hazy/vague. **달빛** moonlight. **점점** gradually. **가까워지다** to get nearer.

Proverb

윗물이 맑아야 아랫물도 맑다.
(Literal) The water of the lower stream is clean only
when the water of the upper stream is clean.
The elder (superior) must be good so that the younger (junior) can follow and be good.

Reading Comprehension Quiz

According to the story, the brothers were jealous of each other.

A. True B. False

The brothers made living selling fruit at a market.

A. True B. False

Which of the brothers got married recently?

A. The Younger Brother B. The Older Brother C. None of Them

The younger brother was happy that he had more rice sheaves than his older brother.

A. True B. False

The brothers were surprised when they woke up in the morning because the rice sheaves were…

A. Gone missing. B. Rotten C. On fire. D. The same.

At first, the brothers doubted their wives as the culprit.

A. True B. False

What is the most likely reaction the brothers had when they found out that it was them who moved the rice sheaves?

A. Anger B. Confusion C. Gratitude D. Doubt

Answer : B / B / A / B / D / B / C

나무 그늘을 산 소년
The Boy Who Bought the Shade of a Tree

옛날 어느 마을에
욕심쟁이 부자 노인이 살았습니다.

욕심쟁이 부자 노인의 집 앞에는
커다란 느티나무가 한 그루 있었습니다.

더운 여름날이면 부자 노인은 시원한 느티나무
아래에서 낮잠을 자곤 했습니다.

그런데 어느 날, 소년이 옆에 와서 앉는 바람에
부자 노인이 잠에서 깨어났습니다.

"이놈! 내 그늘에 왜 마음대로 앉느냐?
당장 꺼져라!"

소년은 깜짝 놀라서 물었어요.

"어떻게 이 나무 그늘이 영감네 것입니까?"
"이 나무는 우리 할아버지가 심으셨다.
그러니 내 것이지, 아니면 누구 거란 말이냐?"

소년은 어안이 벙벙했습니다.
소년은 못된 노인을 골려 주고 싶어졌습니다.

"아이고, 영감! 용서하세요. 제가 잘 몰랐습니다.
그런데 저도 그늘이 필요하니
이 나무 그늘을 저에게 파시겠어요?"

욕심 많은 부자 노인은 귀가 솔깃했습니다.

Once upon a time,
there lived a greedy rich old man in a village.

There was a large zelkova tree in front of the
house of the greedy old man.

On hot summer days, the rich old man used to
take a nap under the cool zelkova tree.

But one day, the rich old man woke up
because a boy came and sat next to him.

"You brat! Why are you sitting in my shade?
Beat it right now!"

The boy was surprised and asked.

"How can the shade of this tree
belong to you?"
"This tree was planted by my grandfather.
So, it's mine, or whose is it?"

The boy was dumbfounded.
The boy wanted to tease the wicked old man.

"Oh, my. Sir! Forgive me. I didn't know that.
But since I need shade, too,
would you sell the shade of this tree to me?"

The greedy rich old man was tempted to listen.

““좋아, 그러나 나중에
되돌려 달라고 하면 안되네!”
“예, 걱정하지 마십시오. 얼마면 되겠습니까?”
“흠, 닷 냥은 받아야겠네.”

소년에게 닷 냥은 아주 큰 돈이었습니다.
하지만 소년은 이내 돈을 마련해 돌아왔습니다.

시간이 지나고 해가 지기 시작했습니다.
그러자 나무 그림자가 서서히 부자 노인의 집
마당으로 길게 펼쳐지기 시작했습니다.

소년은 냉큼 일어나서 나무 그늘을 따라,
부자 노인 집 마당으로 자리를 옮겼습니다
.

해가 더 지자, 나무 그늘은
안방까지 닿았습니다. 소년은 안방에 들어가
드러누웠습니다.

“이야! 그늘이 참 시원하구나!”
“이놈이 이젠 내 집 안방까지 올라오네.
어서 썩 꺼지거라!”
“영감, 저는 제가 돈을 주고 산 나무의 그늘을
따라왔을 뿐입니다.”

부자 노인은 할 말이 없었습니다.
그 뒤로도 소년은 부자 노인 집을
제집 드나들 듯했습니다.

마을 사람들도 초대해서
그늘에 함께 앉았습니다.

결국 부자 노인은 집을 버리고
멀리 떠났습니다. 소년은 그 집에서 사람들이
맘 놓고 쉴 수 있게 했습니다.

"Okay, but you can't ask me to return it later!"
"Yes, don't worry. How much would it be?"
"Hmm, I should get 5 *nyang*."

For the boy, 5 *nyang* was a lot of money.
But the boy soon prepared the money and
came back.

As time passed, the sun began to set. Then the
shadow of the tree gradually began to spread
out into the yard of the rich old man's house.

The boy quickly got up and moved to the yard
of the rich old man's house following the
shade of the tree.

As the sun went further, the shade of the tree
reached the main room. The boy entered the
master bedroom and laid down.

"Wow! The shade is so cool!"
"This brat is coming up to my bedroom now.
Beat it right now!"
"Sir, I just followed the shade of the tree
I paid for."

The rich old man had nothing to say.
Even after that, the boy come in and out of the
rich old man's house as if it were his.

He also invited fellow villagers to sit together
in the shade.

Eventually, the rich old man abandoned his
house and moved far away. The boy allowed
people to relax and make themselves at home
in the house.

Culture Note

Traditionally, Korean society is based on Confucianism. Among them, respecting the elderly has been considered one of the most important virtues. However, this sometimes creates unreasonable situations. An example is an argument that you have to do as the older person says. You can see it in this story, where a rich old man makes unreasonable demands to a young boy. Thanks to the clever boy's spirit, the greedy old man was humiliated and hopefully learned a good lesson.

Vocabulary

커다란 big/large. **느티나무** a zelkova tree. **그루** a stump. / a counter word for trees. **시원한** cool. **낮잠** a nap. **옆** side. **앉다** to sit. **바람에** due to/because of. **깨어나다** to wake up. **마음대로** as one pleases/at will. **꺼져라** beat it! **소년** a boy. **어떻게** how. **영감** (formal) an old man. **아니면** if not. **어안이 벙벙하다** dumbfounded. **못된** mean/evil-minded. **골려주다** to tease. **아이고** oh my! **귀가 솔깃하다** is tempted. **냥** a Korean currency unit used in the past. **이내** soon/promptly. **마련하다** to procure. **서서히** gradually. **냉큼** right away/at once. **일어나다** to stand up. **자리** space/place/spot. **옮기다** to move. **안방** master bedroom. **드러눕다** to lie down/sprawl out. **제집** one's house. **초대하다** to invite. **버리다** to throw away/let go. **맘 놓다** to make oneself at home/to be at ease.

Proverb

만사가 욕심대로라면 하늘에다 집도 짓겠다.
(Literal) If everything goes according to your greed, you can build a house in the sky.
It means to be wary of excessive greed because you can't have everything your way.

Reading Comprehension Quiz

Based on the story, the tree provides large enough shade to cover more than one person.

A. True B. False

The greedy old man woke up from a nap because the boy…

A. Made a loud noise. B. Accidentally stepped on him. C. Sat next to him.
D. Brought friends with him.

According to the story, the greedy old man bought the tree from his grandfather.

A. True B. False

According to the story, the boy pretended to believe what the greedy old man claimed to…

A. Show respect. B. Teach him a lesson. C. Build a treehouse.
D. Have him adopt him as his son.

According to the story, the greedy old was __________ by the boy's reaction to his offer to sell the shade for 5 nyang.

A. Furious B. Humiliated C. Tempted D. Scared

According to the story, the boy never intended to buy the shade from the greedy old man.

A. True B. False

What was the most likely emotion the greedy old man had when he left his house?

A. Peaceful B. Proud C. Rewarding D. Regretful

Answer : A / C / B / B / C / B / D

도깨비 요술 방망이와 개암
The Goblin's Magic Club and the Hazelnut

옛날 옛적 어느 마을에 형제가 살았어요.

Once upon a time, two brothers lived in a village.

게으른 형은 일을 하나도 안 했어요.

The older brother didn't work at all.

모든 일은 늘,
착하고 부지런한 동생이 다 했어요.

The kind and diligent younger brother always did all the work.

어느 날,

One day,

동생이 산에 올라가서 나무를 베는데,
나무에서 개암이 떨어졌어요.

the younger brother climbed a mountain and was cutting down trees, and hazelnuts fell from the tree.

동생은 개암을 보고 좋아할 형을 생각하며
주머니 가득 넣었어요.

The younger brother saw hazelnuts and filled his pocket thinking about his older brother who would like them.

여기저기 떨어진 개암을 줍다 보니
어느새 날이 어두워졌어요.

As he picked up the hazelnuts that fell here and there, it suddenly got dark.

그래서 동생은 길을 잃었어요.

So the younger brother got lost.

허둥지둥 길을 찾던 동생은
오두막 한 채를 보았어요.

The younger brother, who was in a hurry to find his way, saw a cabin.

그 오두막에는 아무도 없었어요.

There was no one in the cabin.

"여기서 하룻밤 자고,
날이 밝으면 산에서 내려가야겠다."

*'I'll sleep here overnight and go down from the
mountain when the sun comes up.*

동생은 오두막으로 들어가
벽에 기대어 앉았어요.

The younger brother entered the cabin and sat
against the wall.

눈이 감기려는 순간,
시끄러운 소리가 들렸어요.

The moment his eyes were about to close,
he heard a loud noise.

깜짝 놀라서 문틈으로 살펴보았더니,
도깨비들이 집으로
성큼성큼 다가오고 있었어요.

He was surprised and looked through the
door, and goblins were approaching the house
with big strides.

동생은 후다닥 벽장으로 숨었어요.

The younger brother quickly hid in the closet.

도깨비들이 마당에 모였어요.

The goblins gathered in the yard.

그리고 방망이로 바닥을 내려치자,
보물과 음식이 쏟아져 나왔어요.

And when they hit the floor with a magic
goblin club, treasures and food poured out.

음식을 보자 동생은
배가 고파졌어요.

Upon seeing the food, the younger brother
became hungry.

'아 참, 개암이 있었지!'

Oh, right. I have hazelnuts!

동생은 개암을 꺼내
입에 넣었어요.

The younger brother took out the hazelnuts
and put them in his mouth.

그리고 살짝 깨물었더니,
개암 깨지는 소리가 크게 났어요.

And when he bit it a little, it made a loud
crackling sound.

"어이구, 집이 무너지려나 보다!"

"Oh, my, the house is about to collapse!"

놀란 도깨비들은 허둥지둥 달아났어요.

The surprised goblins rushed away.

오두막에는
도깨비들이 두고 간 보물과 음식,
그리고 도깨비방망이가 있었어요.

In the cabin,
there were treasures, food,
and magic goblin club left behind.

동생은 날이 밝자,

When day broke,

보물과 도깨비방망이를 가지고
집으로 돌아왔어요.

the younger brother returned home with
treasures and a magic goblin club.

지난밤 산에서 있었던 이야기를 들은 형은,
산으로 올라갔어요.

When the older brother heard about last night's
story in the mountain, he went up to the
mountain.

산에 도착하자마자 형은
주머니가 터지도록 개암을 주웠어요.

As soon as the older brother arrived on the
mountain, he picked up hazelnuts to the point
his pockets would burst open.

그리고 형은 벽장에 들어가서
밤이 되기를 기다렸어요.

And the older brother went into the closet and
waited for night to come.

멀리 도깨비들이 오는 소리가 들리자마자 형은,
개암을 입안 가득 넣고 깨물었어요.

As soon as he heard the goblins coming from
afar, he put the hazelnuts in his mouth and bit
them.

그런데,

However,

이번에는 도깨비들이
벽장문을 벌컥 열어젖혔어요.

this time, the goblins flung opened
the closet door.

"감히 우리 도깨비방망이를 훔쳐 가다니!"

"How dare you steal our club!"

형은 도깨비들에게
두들겨 맞았어요.

The older brother was beaten up by the
goblins.

형은 절뚝거리며
간신히 집으로 돌아왔어요.

The older brother barely made it back home
limping.

그날부터 형은 정신을 차렸어요.

From that day on, he learned a lesson.

그리고, 힘든 일도 아우와 함께하면서
사이 좋게 살았어요.

And he lived a good life with his younger
brother even doing the difficult work together.

Culture Note

Unlike the scary goblins in Western folk tales, goblins in Korean traditional folk tales show a lot of similarities with people. Sometimes they are silly, mean, scared, but affectionate. The goblins in this story lost their magic club because they were scared but were able to punish the greedy older brother who came to steal it again. The moral of the story is that excessive greed can bring misfortune.

Vocabulary

게으른 lazy. **나무를 베다** to cut down a tree. **개암** hazelnut. **주머니** a pocket.

여기저기 here and there. **어느새** already/so soon/without one's knowledge.

길을 잃다 to be lost (in direction). **허둥지둥** hurriedly/hastily. **여기** here.

하룻밤 one night. **벽** a wall. **기대다** to lean against.

감기다 to be closed/shut down. **순간** a moment. **시끄러운** loud/noisy.

문틈 a crevice in the door. **살펴보다** to observe/look around.

성큼성큼 with big strides. **후다닥** quickly/nimbly.

벽장 a (built-in/wall) closet. **숨다** to hide. **모이다** to gather/get together.

방망이 a bat/club. **내려치다** to hit/strike/smash.

쏟아져 나오다 to pour/spew out. **깨물다** to bite.

무너지다 to fall down/collapse. **열어젖히다** to fling open. **감히** dare.

두들겨 맞다 to get beat up. **절뚝거리다** to limp. **간신히** barely.

정신을 차리다 to come to senses/consciousness/learn a lesson.

Proverb

남의 떡이 더 커보인다.
(Literal) Others' rice cakes look bigger.
The grass is always greener on the other side of the fence.

Reading Comprehension Quiz

According to the story, the older brother didn't work at all because he was...

A. Disabled B. Married with kids. C. Too old. D. Lazy

Based on the story, we can assume that the older brother likes hazelnuts.

A. True B. False

According to the story, the younger brother spent a lot of time picking up the hazelnuts.

A. True B. False

The younger brother got lost because...

A. He was too focused on picking up the hazelnuts.
B. He didn't know what time it was.
C. He had never been to the mountain before.
D. There was no one around to help him.

The younger brother knew that the house belonged to the goblins.

A. True B. False

The older brother knew that the house belonged to the goblins.

A. True B. False

According to the story, the goblins must have thought that the older brother was the one who stole their magic club.

A. True B. False

Answer : D / A / A / A / B / A / A

자신을 도둑맞은 도령
The Young Bachelor Who Got Himself Stolen

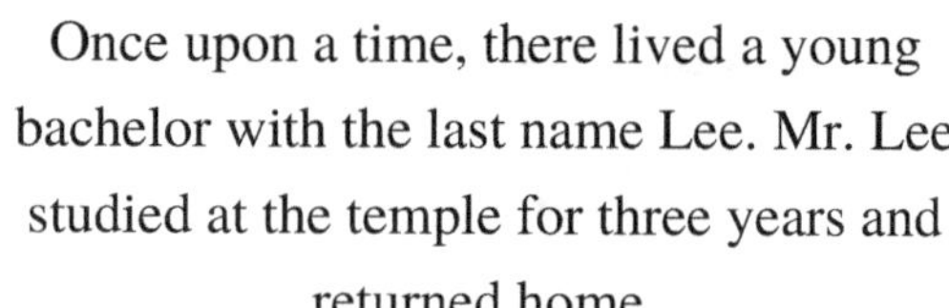

옛날에 이씨 성을 가진 한 도령이 살았습니다. 이 도령은 절에서 삼 년 동안 공부를 하고 집으로 돌아왔습니다.

Once upon a time, there lived a young bachelor with the last name Lee. Mr. Lee studied at the temple for three years and returned home.

그런데 이 도령은 집에 돌아와서 깜짝 놀랐습니다.

However, Mr. Lee was surprised when he returned home.

자기와 똑같은 모습을 한 사람이 있었기 때문입니다. 그런데 그 도령도 자기가 진짜 이 도령이라고 주장했습니다.

It's because there was someone who looked the same as him, but that bachelor also claimed that he was the real Mr. Lee.

두 사람이 이렇게 다투고 있자, 이 도령의 부모님이 나왔습니다.

When the two were arguing like this, Mr. Lee's parents came out.

부모님은 누가 진짜 이 도령인지 알기 위해 여러 가지 질문을 했습니다. 하지만 두 사람은 모두 똑같이 대답하였습니다.

The parents asked them several questions to find out who the real Mr. Lee was. But both of them answered the same.

그러던 중 어머니가,

Then the mother asked,

"지난해에 밥상을 새로 만들었는데 어떤 나무로 만들었느냐?"라고 물었습니다.

"I made a new table last year. What kind of wood was it made of?"

가짜 이 도령은 대답했지만 진짜 이 도령은 대답하지 못했습니다. 작년에 절간에서 공부하고 있었기 때문에 알 수 없었던 것입니다.

The fake Mr. Lee replied, but the real Mr. Lee failed to answer. He couldn't know because he was studying at a temple last year.

그런데 오히려, 부모님은 진짜 이 도령이
가짜라고 생각하고 쫓아냈습니다.

But rather, the parents thought the
real Mr. Lee was fake and kicked him out.

집에서 쫓겨난 이 도령은 어느 날,
한 스님을 만나게 되었습니다.

One day, Mr. Lee, who was kicked out of
the house, met a monk.

이 도령은 스님에게 자초지종을 설명했습니다.

Mr. Lee explained the whole story
to the monk.

스님은 그 이유를 알고 있었습니다.
그것은 바로 이 도령이 절에서 공부할 때
아무 데나 깎아 버린 손톱 때문이었습니다.

The monk knew the reason. It was because
of Mr. Lee's fingernails that he cut and left
everywhere when he studied at the temple.

이 손톱을 주워 먹은 들쥐가
가짜 이 도령으로 변신한것이었습니다.
손톱에는 그 사람의 혼이 들어있기 때문에
마음과 모습을 훔칠 수 있었다고 말했습니다.

The field mouse that ate these nails turned
into a fake Mr. Lee. He said it was able to
steal his mind and appearance because the
nails contain the person's soul.

스님은 가짜 이 도령을 쫓아낼 수 있는 방법을
알려주었습니다. 진짜 이 도령은
스님이 준 고양이와 함께 집으로 돌아갔습니다.

The monk told him how to kick out the fake
Mr. Lee. The real Mr. Lee headed back
home with a cat given tp him by the monk.

진짜 이 도령은 집으로 돌아와
큰 소리로 가짜 이 도령을 불렀습니다.
그리고, 가짜 도령의 앞에 고양이를 내놓았습니다.
그러자, 고양이는 가짜 도령에게 달려들었습니다.

The real Mr. Lee returned home and called
the fake Mr. Lee out loud.
And, he put the cat in front of the fake Mr.
Then, the cat rushed to the fake Mr.

그러자 가짜 도령은 비명을 지르며
땅바닥에 쓰러졌습니다.
그리고 커다란 들쥐로 변했습니다.

Then the fake Mr. fell to the ground
screaming.
And it turned into a large field mouse.

이 도령의 부모님은 이 모습을 보고
깜짝 놀랐습니다.

Mr. Lee's parents were startled to see this.

그제야 진짜 이 도령과 부모님은
서로를 반길 수 있었답니다.

Only then could young Mr. Lee and his
parents greet each other.

Culture Note

This story contains an interesting superstition that Koreans believe in. It is a belief that "you shouldn't cut your nails in the late evening," because if you cut your nails in the dark at night, the mouse that eats them becomes a human. The creepy superstition is said to have been created to prevent children from getting hurt while cutting their nails at night when there was no electricity. It is interesting to learn how Koreans lived in the past through superstition.

Vocabulary

이씨 성 A Mr./Mrs.with the last name Lee (이 = Lee, 씨 = affix meaning "Mr./Mrs." 성 = last name" 도령 (formal) a bachelor/youth.

절/절간 a Buddhist temple. 공부 study. 진짜 real(ity).

주장하다 to assert/claim. 다투다 to quarrel/argue. 새로 newly/freshly.

만들다 to make/build. 알 수 없다 not able to know. 오히려 rather/instead.

쫓아내다 to chase away/kick out. 가짜 fake. 스님 (honorific) a monk.

자초지종 all the details/complete account (of). 아무 데나 wherever/anywhere.

깎다 to cut/clip/carve. 버리다 to throw away/dump. 손톱 toenail.

들쥐 wild/field rat. 혼 soul/spirit. 들어있다 is inside/contained.

방법 a method/means. 고양이 a cat. 내놓다 to put/take out.

달려들다 to attack/charge at/spring out at. 비명 지르다 to scream/shriek.

반기다 to greet/welcome.

Proverb

힘쓰기보다 꾀쓰기가 낫다.
(Literal) It's better to use your brain than to use force.
It's better taking shortcuts than running.
It means that you can solve difficult problems more easily with wisdom
rather than with force.

Reading Comprehension Quiz

According to the story, the bachelor was expecting to see someone who looks exactly the same as him.

A. True B. False

The bachelor's parents actually knew who the real son was but asked a set of questions nonetheless.

A. True B. False

The fake bachelor could answer the mother's question while the real bachelor couldn't because…

A. He was smarter than the real one. B. He read the mother's mind.
C. He lived in the house while the real one was away. D. He studied harder.

The parents kicked the real bachelor out of the house because…

A. They wanted to save his life. B. He couldn't answer the question.
C. He wasn't a filial son. D. They only wanted one son.

According to the story, the fake bachelor came into being during the time the real bachelor was studying at a temple.

A. True B. False

The cat jumped at the fake bachelor because…

A. It knew he was a fake. B. It knew it was a mouse. C. It hates people.
D. The monk ordered it to.

According to the story, the cat could see what the parents couldn't.

A. True B. False

Answer : B / B / C / B / A / B / A

산신령에게 밀가루 소 백마리를 바친 농부
The Farmer Who Offered a Hundred Flour Cows to the Mountain Spirit

옛날 어느 한 마을에 가난한 농부가
살고 있었습니다. 그 농부는 병에 걸렸지만,
돈이 없어서 약을 살 수 없었어요.

Once upon a time, there lived a poor farmer in a village. The farmer got sick, but he couldn't buy medicine because he didn't have money.

하지만 가족들을 위해서
하루라도 일을 멈출 수가 없었습니다.

But he couldn't stop working even for a day for his family.

그러던 어느 날 농부는 산으로 올라가
삼일 동안 간절히 기도했습니다.

Then one day, the farmer went up to the mountain and prayed earnestly for three days.

삼일째 되던 날,
동굴 깊은 곳에서 목소리가 들려왔습니다.

On the third day, a voice came from deep in the cave.

"가련한 농부여, 너의 간절한 기도를 들었노라."

"Poor farmer, I heard your earnest prayer."

농부의 기도를 들은
산신령이 나타난 것이었습니다.

The mountain spirit who heard the farmer's prayer appeared.

농부가 말했습니다.

The farmer said,

"산신령님, 저의 병을 낫게 해주신다면
소 백마리를 드리겠습니다."

"Mountain Spirit, if you can heal my illness, I'll give you 100 cows."

농부의 약속을 믿은 산신령은
농부의 병을 낫게 해주었습니다.

The mountain spirit, who believed in the farmer's promise, healed the farmer's illness.

병이 나은 농부는 고민에 빠졌습니다.
농부는 꾀를 내었습니다.

The farmer who got better was in trouble. The farmer thought of a ploy.

농부는 밀가루 사용해
가짜 소 백마리를 만들었습니다.

그리고 산신령과 약속한 곳으로 갔습니다.

"약속대로 소 백마리를 바치옵니다."

하지만 산신령은 농부가
속임수를 쓰는 것을 알았어요.

화가 난 산신령은 농부에게 말했습니다.

"너의 정성에 감동하였으니
은돈 오십냥을 주겠다.
내일 아침 일찍 바닷가로 나가거라."

농부는 다음 날 아침 일찍
산신령이 이야기해 준
바닷가로 나갔습니다.

'은돈 오십냥이 어디 있을까?'
농부는 두리번거렸습니다.

하지만 바로 그때, 해적들이 나타나
농부를 배에 태운 뒤
먼 나라로 떠났습니다.

해적들은 농부를 은돈 오십냥에
노예로 팔아버렸습니다.

농부는,

'아, 내 몸값이 은돈 오십냥이었던 것이로구나'

하며 약속을 지키지 않고 거짓말한 것을
후회했습니다.

The farmer made 100 fake cows using flour.

And he went to the place he promised with
the mountain spirit.

"I offer 100 cows as promised."

But the mountain spirit found out that the
farmer was cheating.

The angry mountain spirit told the farmer,

"I'm touched by your sincerity, so I'll give
you 50 *nyang* of silver coins. Go out to the
beach early tomorrow morning."

The farmer went out to the beach the
mountain spirit told him about,
early in the next morning.

Where is the 50 nyang of silver coins?
The farmer looked around.

But just then, pirates appeared, put the
farmer on a boat, and left for a distant
country.

The pirates sold the farmer as a slave for
50 *nyang* of silver coins.

The farmer thought,

Oh, my ransom was 50 nyang of silver coins.

And regretted lying instead of keeping his
promise.

Culture Note

Through this story, you can see the traditional shamanism beliefs of Koreans, where the image of a weak human being gets punished for trying to deceive the almighty mountain spirit. It's the Korean people's idea of adapting to nature and living according to divine providence. Above all, it stresses the importance of keeping promises.

Vocabulary

약 medicine. 하루라도 just for even one day. 간절히 earnestly. 기도하다 to pray. 동굴 a cave. 가련한 pitiful/pathetic. 낫게 하다 to heal (someone). 백 one hundred. 믿다 to believe/trust. 고민 a concern/worry. 밀가루 flour. 바치다 to offer/dedicate. 속임수 a trickery/deception. 은돈 silver money. 은 means "silver" and 돈 means "money". 내일 tomorrow. 바닷가 seaside. 두리번거리다 to look around. 해적 a pirate. 나라 a nation/country. 노예 a slave. 팔다 to sell. 몸값 ransom. 몸 means "body" and 값 means "price".

Proverb

열 길 물속은 알아도 한 길 사람의 속은 모른다.
(Literal) You might know what's in ten *gil* (Korean measurement, about the height of an adult) of water, but you do not know what's in one *gil* of a man.
Man and melons are hard to know.
It means that one should be careful not to blindly trust someone because one's mind cannot be known from the outside.

Reading Comprehension Quiz

According to the story, the farmer had to keep working although he was ill because...

A. He couldn't afford medication. B. He had to support his family.
C. He'd die if he stopped working. D. He had a lot of debt.

According to the story, the farmer seems to believe in supernatural beings.

A. True B. False

According to the mountain spirit, the farmer's prayer was heard because...

A. He prayed for three days. B. He was honest. C. His prayer was earnest.
D. He had a loud voice.

Based on the story, the farmer believed it was worth offering a hundred cows to save his life.

A. True B. False

The mountain spirit got furious because...

A. He doesn't like flour. B. He figured out that the farmer was lying. C. The farmer brought less than a hundred cows. D. He expected more than a hundred cows.

Based on the reaction of the farmer, we can assume that he didn't think the mountain spirit was angry.

A. True B. False

Based on the story, the farmer was regretful that...

A. He was only worth fifty silver coins. B. He wasn't strong enough to beat the pirates. C. He only offered fifty cows. D. He didn't keep his promise.

Answer : B / A / C / A / B / A / D

새 망태기 헌 망태기
The New Mesh Bag and the Old Mesh Bag

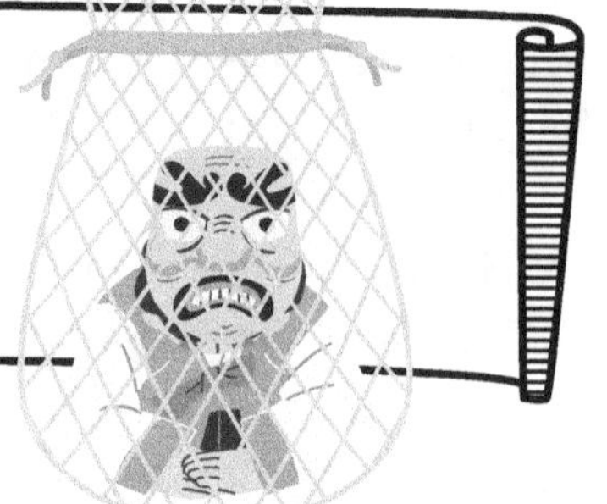

옛날 어느 마을에 형제가 살고 있었습니다.
형은 마음씨가 나빴지만,
아우는 마음씨가 아주 착했습니다.

형제의 아버지는 자신이 죽으면
형제가 재산을 나누어 가지라고 당부했습니다.

그러나 아버지가 죽고 나자
욕심 많은 형은
아우를 내쫓아버리고
재산을 혼자서 차지했습니다.

집에서 쫓겨나온 아우는
산에서 나무를 베다가
사냥꾼을 만났습니다.

사냥꾼은 아우에게 돈벌이를 함께 해보자고
했습니다. 아우는 그렇게 하기로 했습니다.

다음 날 저녁, 사냥꾼과 아우는
산속으로 들어갔습니다.

사냥꾼은 새 망태기를 나뭇가지에 매달고,
아우에게 들어가라고 했습니다.

Once upon a time, two brothers lived in a village. The older brother was evil-hearted, but the younger brother was very kind-hearted.

The brothers' father advised the brothers to share their property when he died.

However, after his father died, the greedy brother kicked out his younger brother and took over the property by himself.

The younger brother, who was kicked out of the house, met a hunter while cutting down trees in the mountain.

The hunter asked the younger brother to make money together. The younger brother decided to do so.

The next evening, the hunter and the younger brother went into the mountain.

The hunter hung a new mesh bag from a branch and asked the younger brother to get inside.

그리고는 주변에 날카로운 창과 칼을
거꾸로 꽂아 두었습니다.

밤이 되자 큰 호랑이 한 마리가
먹이를 찾으러 나왔습니다.

호랑이는 나무에 매달린 망태기 속에 있는
아우를 발견했어요.

그래서 망태기를 향해 뛰어올랐습니다.
하지만 창과 칼에 찔린 호랑이는 피를 흘리며
쓰러졌습니다.

아우와 사냥꾼은 호랑이 가죽을
팔아서 큰 부자가 되었습니다.

아우가 큰 부자가 되었다는 소식을 들은 형은
샘이 났습니다. 그래서 사냥꾼의 집에 찾아가서
자신과 함께 사냥하자고 졸랐습니다.

사냥꾼은 지금 가진 것은 헌 망태기뿐이라고
말했습니다. 하지만 형은 부자가 될 욕심에
눈이 멀어서, 그래도 괜찮다고 했습니다.

결국 사냥꾼은 헌 망태기를 나뭇가지에 매달았고,
형은 그 안에 들어가서 호랑이를 기다렸습니다.

밤이 되자 호랑이가 망태기를 보고
뛰어올랐습니다. 그런데 그때, 헌 망태기 끈이
끊어졌습니다.

욕심 많은 형은 호랑이 밥이 되었습니다.

Then he planted sharp spears and swords
upside down around it.

As night came, a big tiger came out to find
food.

The tiger found the younger brother in the
mesh bag hanging from a tree.

So it jumped toward the mesh bag.
However, the tiger, stabbed with a spear and
knife, fell bleeding.

The younger brother and the hunter became
rich by selling the tiger's skin.

When the older brother heard that his
younger brother became rich, he was jealous
of him. So he went to the hunter's house and
begged him to hunt with him.

The hunter said that all he has now is an old
mesh bag. But the older brother was blinded
by the desire to be rich, so he said it was
okay.

Eventually, the hunter hung an old mesh bag
from a branch, and the older brother went
inside and waited for the tiger.

As night came, the tiger jumped up when it
saw the mesh bag. But at that moment, the
string of the old mesh bag snapped.

The greedy older brother
became a meal for the tiger.

Culture Note

In this story set in traditional Korea, a paternal society, the eldest son is depicted as selfish despite inheriting all of his parents' wealth. On the contrary, a brother who works hard without complaining is depicted as a good character. Here, a tiger, which Koreans think is a mystic creature, appears to punish the evil character. Through these dynamics, you can learn the importance of sharing, wit, and loving each other without being overly greedy.

Vocabulary

아버지 father. **죽다** to die. **재산** asset/property. **당부하다** to request/plea.
차지하다 to take up/occupy. **사냥꾼** a hunter. **사냥** means "hunting" and 꾼 means "someone who does it". **돈벌이** making/earning money.
새 (1) new. (2) a bird. **망태기** a mesh bag. **매달다** to hang/dangle.
주변 around/surroundings. **날카로운** sharp. **창** a spear.**칼** a knife.
거꾸로 upside down. **꽂아두다** to put/stick in. **먹이** prey/feed.
뛰어오르다 to jump/leap (up). **피** blood. **흘리다** to spill/drop. **가죽** leather.
샘이 나다 to be jealous. **조르다** to nag/press/nag. **헌** old/worn out.
눈이 멀다 to become blind. **끈** a string. **끊어지다** to snap/be cut.

Proverb

허욕에 들뜨면 한 치 앞도 못 본다.
(Literal) If you're excited by vanity, you can't see an inch ahead.
It means that if you are excited by vain greed,
you will not be able to make rational judgments.

Reading Comprehension Quiz

According to the story, the older brother honored the father's will.

A. True B. False

The older brother took all of the deceased father's bequest because he was…

A. Secretly told to. B. In need of a lot of money. C. Greedy D. Worried about his younger brother.

Based on the story, we can assume that the younger brother and the hunter both needed money.

A. True B. False

The younger brother agreed to go into the mesh bag although he didn't want to.

A. True B. False

According to the story, the tiger jumped at the mesh bag even though it knew that there were spears and knives.

A. True B. False

According to the story, the hunter didn't keep the promise he made with the younger brother.

A. True B. False

According to the story, the mesh bag in which the older brother was in snapped because…

A. The tiger took a bite at it. B. It was old. C. The branch wasn't strong enough. D. The hunter didn't tie it well.

Answer : B / C / A / B / B / B / B

삼 년 고개
The Three-Year Hill

아주 먼 옛날, 어느 마을에는
한 번 넘어지면 삼 년밖에 못 산다는
전설이 있는 고개가 있었어요.

사람들은 이 고개를 '삼 년 고개'라고 부르며
고개를 지날 때마다 넘어지지 않게 조심했어요.

심지어 거북이처럼 기어가는 사람도 있었어요.

그러던 어느 날, 머리가 하얀 할아버지가
삼 년 고개를 조심스럽게 넘고 있었어요.

그런데 수풀에서 토끼가 튀어나왔어요.
깜짝 놀란 할아버지는 뒤로 넘어졌어요.

"아이고 삼 년밖에 못 살겠구나..."
할아버지는 슬프게 울었어요.

어느덧 삼 년째가 되었어요.
할아버지는 살날이 며칠 남지 않았다는 생각에
걱정이 가득했어요.

마을에서 가장 용하다는 의원이 찾아왔어요.
하지만 무슨 병인지 전혀 몰라서
고칠 수 없었어요.

A very long time ago, in a village, there was a hill with a legend that says once you fall down from the hill, you can only live for three years.

People called this hill the "Three-Year Hill" and were careful not to fall every time they passed it.

There were even people crawling like a turtle.

Then one day, a grandfather with white hair was carefully crossing the Three-Year Hill.

But a rabbit jumped out of the bushes. The surprised grandfather fell backward.

"Oh, I can only live for three years..."
The grandfather cried sadly.

It's already the third year.
The grandfather was worried that there were only a few days left to live.

The most skilled doctors in the village visited, but they couldn't cure him because they had no idea what kind of illness it was.

다음 날, 어린 손자가 할아버지를 찾아왔어요.

"할아버지, 어쩌다 병이 나신 거예요?"
라고 물었어요.

"삼 년 고개에서 넘어졌단다.
살날이 얼마 남지 않아서
몸에 힘이 하나도 없구나"

"할아버지, 한 번 넘어지면 삼 년이니까,
두 번 넘어지면 육 년,
세 번 넘어지면 구 년을 사실 거예요!"

"그렇지!"

할아버지는 곧장 삼 년 고개로 달려갔어요.

그러고는 일부러 계속 넘어지기 시작했어요.

"넘어질수록 오래 사니까, 계속 굴러보자!"

할아버지는 계속해서 넘어졌습니다.

더 이상 걱정이 없어진 할아버지는,
그 후로도 오래오래 건강하게 살았어요.

그리고 마을 사람들도 그 소식을 듣고
모두 삼 년 고개에서 넘어졌어요.

그때부터 '삼 년 고개'는 '장수 고개'가 되었어요.

The next day, a young grandson visited his
grandfather.

He asked, "Grandpa, how did you get sick?"

"I fell down at the Three-year Hill.
I don't have much time left to live so I don't
have any strength in my body."

"Grandpa, it's three years if you fall down
once, so six years if you fall down twice,
and nine years if you fall down three times!"

"Right!"

Grandfather ran straight to the
Three-year Hill.

Then he kept falling down on purpose.

"The more you fall down, the longer you
live. Let's keep rolling!"

The grandfather kept falling down. The
grandfather, who had no more worries, lived
healthily for a long time after that.

And when the villagers heard the news, they
all fell down from the Three-year Hill.

Since then, the "Three-Year Hill" has
become the "Longevity Hill".

Culture Note

Like the witty grandson who cured his grandfather's illness, the lesson of this story is that it is important to think positively because, if you change your thoughts positively even for a moment, what you were once scared of may not seem like a big deal.

Vocabulary

전설 legend. 고개 (1) a hill. (2) the head. 부르다 to call.

조심하다 to practice caution/be careful/be beware. 거북이 a turtle.

기어가다 to crawl. 하얀 white. 수풀 forest/the woods. It's a variation of 숲.

넘어지다 to fall down/collapse. 어느덧 already/so soon. 고치다 to fix/repair/heal (an illness). 어린 young/little. 손자 a grandson/grandchild.

힘 power/strength. 오래 long/a long time.

더 이상 (followed by a negative statement) not anymore.

그때부터 from/since the/that moment.

Proverb

긁어 부스럼 만든다
(Literal) To scratch something into a boil.
Borrowing trouble. / If it's not broken, don't fix it.
It means you are making a situation worse than it is
by doing something you didn't have to do.

Reading Comprehension Quiz

According to the story, people believed that the legend was scientifically proven.

A. True B. False

Some people crawled like a turtle to make sure that they…

A. Don't walk too fast. B. Don't upset the mountain spirit. C. Don't fall.
D. Show respect to the turtle spirit.

Based on the story, we can guess that the grandfather was afraid of the rabbit.

A. True B. False

What was the most likely reason doctor couldn't tell what the problem was?

A. The grandfather wouldn't tell what happened.
B. The grandfather refused treatment.
C. The doctor didn't bring the necessary tools.
D. The symptoms were not visible to the doctor.

According to the story, the grandson knew how to cure his grandfather's illness because he also had the same illness before.

A. True B. False

The grandson suggested his grandfather keep falling to make fun of him.

A. True B. False

The most probable cause of the illness is…

A. Stress B. Greed C. Guilt D. Malnutrition

Answer : B / C / B / D / B / B / A

옹고집전
The Tale of Mr. Stubborn

옛날 한양에 옹고집이라 불리우는 사람이
살고 있었습니다. 옹고집은 재물이 많아서
큰 집에 살았습니다.

Once upon a time, there lived a person called
Mr. Stubborn in Hanyang. Mr. Stubborn lived
in a big house because he had a lot of wealth.

그럼에도 불구하고 옹고집은
불쌍한 사람을 도와본 적이 한 번도 없었습니다.

Nevertheless, Mr. Stubborn never helped poor
people.

그러던 어느 날 옹고집의 집에
스님이 찾아왔습니다. 스님은 대문 앞에서
염불을 외우면서 시주를 부탁했습니다.
그러자 하인이 나와서,

Then one day, a monk came to Mr. Stubborn's
house. The monk asked for an offering while
reciting the Buddhist prayer in front of the
gate. Then, a servant came out.

"우리 주인께서 알면 큰일 납니다.
어서 돌아가십시오" 하고 말했습니다.

"You would be in trouble if my master knew.
Go back now," he said.

스님은,

The monk said,

"좋은 일을 하면 좋은 일이 찾아오고
나쁜 일을 하면 나쁜 일이 찾아옵니다"
하며 계속 목탁을 두드렸습니다.

"If you do good things, good things will come,
and if you do bad things, bad things will
come." and continued to beat the wooden bell,

이 대화를 들은 옹고집이
대문을 열고 나왔습니다.
그리고 스님에게 소리쳤습니다.

Upon hearing this conversation, Mr. Stubborn
opened the gate and came out.
And he shouted at the monk.

그리고 하인을 시켜 스님을
몽둥이로 때리게 했습니다.
그리고는 스님을 외양간에 가두었습니다.

And he made a servant hit the monk with a
club. Then he locked the monk in a barn.

그날 밤이 되어서야 옹고집은
스님을 풀어주었습니다.
절로 돌아간 스님은
이상한 부적을 써서 자신의 몸에 붙였습니다.

그러자 스님이 옹고집의 모습으로 변했습니다.
옹고집이 산책을 떠난 사이,
스님은 옹고집의 집으로 가서
옹고집 행세를 하였습니다.

산책을 갔다가 돌아온 옹고집은
집에 들어서며 소리쳤습니다.

"누가 내 집에서 시끄럽게 구느냐!"

그러자 옹고집으로 변신한 스님이

"당신은 누군데 함부로 내 집에 들어와
큰소리를 치는가?" 하고 소리쳤습니다.

하인들과 옹고집의 가족들은
누가 진짜 옹고집인지 도저히 알 수 없었습니다.
그래서 원님을 찾아갔습니다.
원님은 고민 끝에,
진짜 옹고집이 가짜라고 생각했습니다.

결국, 진짜 옹고집은 자신의 집에서 쫓겨나
떠돌이가 되어 구걸하며 살았습니다.
진짜 옹고집은 진심으로 자신의
이기심을 뉘우쳤습니다.

그리고 불쌍한 사람들을 도우며 살았습니다.
이 소식을 들은 스님은 다시 절로 돌아갔고,
진짜 옹고집은 집으로 돌아올 수 있었습니다.

It was not until that night that Mr. Stubborn
released the monk. The monk who returned
to the temple wrote a strange talisman and
attached it to his body.

Then the monk turned into Mr. Stubborn.
While Mr. Stubborn left for a walk, the
monk went to Mr. Stubborn's house and
pretended to be Mr. Stubborn.

Mr. Stubborn, who returned from a walk,
shouted as he entered the house.

"Who is making noise in my house?"

Then the monk who turned into
Mr. Stubborn shouted,

"Who are you to come into my house
and shout loudly?"

The servants and their families could not tell
which was the real Mr. Stubborn.
So they went to the magistrate.
After much consideration, the magistrate
thought that the real Mr. Stubborn was fake.

Eventually, the real Mr. Stubborn was
kicked out of his house and became a
wanderer and lived begging. The real Mr.
Stubborn sincerely regretted his selfishness.

And he lived helping poor people.
Upon hearing this news, the monk went
back to the temple, and the real
Mr. Stubborn was able to return home.

Culture Note

In the past, Korea was a country that worshiped Buddhism along with shamanism beliefs. But in this story, Mr. Stubborn shows the worldly greed and selfishness that Buddhism teaches us to avoid. The monk that appears here acts as a mirror of conscience so that Mr. Stubborn can repent of his faults, just like the old Scrooge in the novel A Christmas Carol. There is only one way to solve the curse, which is to help poor people.

Vocabulary

옹고집 Mr. Stubborn. **고집** means "stubbornness" and **옹** is an emphasizing word. **대문** a gate. **염불** Buddhist prayer. **시주** donation/offering. **하인** a servant. **큰일 나다** to get into trouble/become serious. **일** deed. **목탁** a wooden bell. **대화** a conversation. **부적** a talisman. **붙이다** to attach/affix/put on. **산책** a walk/stroll. **행세를 하다** to pretend as. **함부로** without permission. **도저히** at all. **떠돌이** a wanderer. **구걸하다** to beg/panhandle. **진심** truth/sincerity. **이기심** selfishness. **소식** news/word.

Proverb

찔러도 피 한방울 안 나온다.
(Literal) Not a drop of blood will come out even when pierced.
A figurative expression for someone very cruel or heartless.

Reading Comprehension Quiz

According to the story, Mr. Stubborn couldn't help the poor people because he didn't have enough money.

A. True B. False

According to the story, the monk visited Mr. Stubborn's house to ask him to convert.

A. True B. False

The servant knew that his master would get upset because…

A. He doesn't like monks. B. He doesn't like sharing.
 C. He doesn't have money. D. He doesn't trust the servant.

According to the story, Mr. Stubborn believed in Buddha's teachings.

A. True B. False

Based on the story, the monk put a strange talisman on his body to heal the wounds from getting beaten.

A. True B. False

After turning into Mr. Stubborn, the monk stole Mr. Stubborn's belongings.

A. True B. False

The real Mr. Stubborn could go back to his house because…

A. He made a large donation to the monk. B. He helped other people.
C. The magistrate ordered so. D. The monk died.

Answer : B / B / B / B / B / B / B

큰 바위 재판
The Big Rock Trial

옛날에 비단 장수가 있었어요.
어느 날, 그는 비단을 짊어지고 시골길을 걸어가고 있었어요.

Once upon a time, there was a silk seller. One day, he was walking on a country road carrying silk.

비단 장수는 지쳐서 큰 바위 앞에서 잠깐 쉬었어요. 그러다가 깜빡 잠들었어요.

The silk seller was tired and rested for a while in front of a big rock. And then he dozed off.

하지만 잠에서 깨어보니 비단 짐이 사라졌어요.

But when he woke up, the silk luggage disappeared.

"아이고, 내 비단이 다 어디 간 거야! 나는 이제 망했구나!'

"Where's all my silk? I'm doomed now!"

비단 장수는 마을 원님을 찾아가 하소연 하였습니다. 원님은 지혜롭기로 유명했어요. 원님은 비단 장수 말을 듣고 한참을 생각했어요. 그리고 말했어요.

The silk seller visited the village magistrate and complained. The magistrate was famous for being wise. The magistrate listened to the silk seller and thought for a long time. And he said,

"주변에 아무도 그 사건을 본 사람이 없으니 큰 바위를 추궁하면 범인을 알 수 있을 것이다! 어서 그 큰 바위를 여기로 데려 오너라!"

"Nobody around you has seen the incident, so if I interrogate the big rock, we will know the culprit! Hurry up and bring the big rock here!"

큰 바위를 재판한다는 소문은 금세 마을 전역에 퍼졌어요.

Rumors of judging a large rock quickly spread throughout the village.

재판 당일 구경꾼들이 몰려들기 시작했어요.

On the day of the trial, spectators began to flock.

원님은 문지기에게 명령하여
옷을 잘 입은 사람들만 들여보내라고
일러 놓았어요.
드디어 큰 바위 재판이 시작되었어요.

“큰 바위 네 이놈!
범인이 누군지 바른대로 말하거라!”

원님은 큰 바위에 호통을 쳤지만
큰 바위는 아무 말도 없었습니다.

구경꾼들은 모두 웃었어요. 원님은,

“감히 재판하는데 웃다니!
웃은 사람들을 모두 옥에 가두어라”
라고 명령했어요.

옥에 갇힌 사람들은 원님에게
용서해 달라고 애원했어요.
원님은 비단을 바치면 풀어주겠다고 말했습니다.

옥에 갇힌 사람들은 비단을 사서
원님에게 바쳤어요.

그 비단은 비단 장수가 잃어버린 비단과
똑같은 것이었어요!

원님이 누구에게서 비단을 샀는지 묻자 모두가
옆 마을 비단 장수에게서 샀다고 말했어요.

원님은 당장 그 비단 장수를 잡아 오라고
명령했어요. 이렇게 해서 비단 장수는
잃어버린 비단을 모두 찾을 수 있었어요.

The magistrate ordered the gatekeeper to let
only well-dressed people in.
Finally, the big rock trial began.

"Big rock, you punk!
Tell us truthfully who the culprit is!"

The magistrate yelled at the big rock,
but the big rock said nothing.

All the spectators laughed.
The magistrate said,

"How dare you laugh during a trial!
Keep all the people who laughed in prison,"
he ordered.

People who were locked in prison begged the
magistrate to forgive them. The magistrate
said he would release them if they offered
silk.

People who were locked in prison bought
their silk and offered it to the magistrate.

The silk was just like the silk that the silk
seller lost!

When the magistrate asked who they bought
the silk from, everyone said they bought it
from a silk dealer in the next village.

The magistrate ordered to catch the silk seller
right away. In this way, the silk seller was
able to find all the lost silk.

Culture Note

Thanks to the wise magistrate, they could catch the criminal who stole silk. The scene of talking to a big rock is ridiculous, but this is where the wisdom of the magistrate stands out. The moral of the story is that those who commit a crime will be punished eventually, even if there is no one watching.

Vocabulary

비단 silk. 장수 a seller. 짊어지다 to carry (on the shoulder/back). 시골길 country road. 바위 a rock. 깜빡 잠들다 to doze off. 짐 luggage. 망하다 to be ruined/doomed/bankrupt. 하소연 to complain/moan about. 사건 an incident. 추궁하다 to interrogate. 범인 a culprit. 재판 a trial. 구경꾼 a spectator. 구경 means "to spectate" and 꾼 means "someone who does something". 문지기 a gatekeeper .일러 놓다 to have someone informed (in advance). 드디어 finally/eventually. 놈 (informal) guy, (offensive) jerk/punk. 바른대로 truthfully. 호통치다 yell/roar/bawl. 옥 jade. 애원하다 to plead/implore/beg.

Proverb

물이 깊어야 물고기가 모인다.
(Literal) Fish gather only when the water is deep.
Meaning that others will follow only when there is great virtue.

Reading Comprehension Quiz

According to the story, the silk seller didn't plan on taking a nap but fell asleep.

A. True B. False

According to the story, the silk was stolen while he was awake.

A. True B. False

The silk seller couldn't notice the thief because the big rock obstructed his view.

A. True B. False

The silk seller decided to see the magistrate because…

A. The magistrate is the owner of the big rock.
B. The silk seller was friends with the magistrate.
C. The magistrate was wise.
D. The silk seller was exhausted.

According to the story, the spectators at the trial thought that the magistrate was…

A. Smart B. Stupid C. Happy D. Hungry

The magistrate put the spectators in jail because they…

A. Were being noisy. B. Laughed during a trial. C. Didn't pay. D. Were late.

Based on the story, did the magistrate believe that the rock would be able to talk?

A. Yes B. No

Answer : A / B / B / C / B / B / B

부엉이를 잡은 젊은이
The Young Man Who Caught An Owl

옛날 옛적, 어느 부자집에
아주 이상한 일이 생겼어요.

Once upon a time, a very strange thing happened to a rich family.

그 집 뒷마당에는 큰 사과나무가 있었어요.
그런데 그 나무에 검은 부엉이가 날아와 울면,
그 집 식구 중 한 명이 죽었어요.

There was a large apple tree in the backyard of the house. But when a black owl flew into the tree and cried, one of the family members died.

부자는 식구를 모두 잃을까 걱정했어요.
그래서 종이에 크게 써서 모두가 볼 수 있게
집 담벼락에 붙였어요.

The rich man was worried about losing all his family members. So he wrote big on paper and stuck it on the wall of the house fence so that everyone could see it.

'검은 부엉이를 잡아주는 총각에게 내 딸을 주고
내 재산의 반을 주겠다.'

I will give my daughter and half of my fortune to the bachelor who catches the black owl.

많은 총각들이 이 것을 보고
부엉이를 잡으려고 했어요.
하지만 아무도 성공하지 못했어요.

Many bachelors saw this and tried to catch the owl. But no one succeeded. Then one day, a young bachelor saw the message on the wall.

그러던 어느 날 어린 총각이
벽에 붙은 글을 보게 되었어요.

어린 총각은 활을 쏴 본 적이 없었어요,
하지만 누구보다 현명했어요.

The young bachelor had never shot a bow, but he was wiser than anyone else.

어린 총각은 좋은 방법을 생각해 냈어요.
그리고 자신만만하게 대문을 두드렸어요.

The young bachelor came up with a good idea. And he knocked on the gate confidently.

"저에게 부엉이를 잡을 좋은 방법이 있습니다."

"I have a good way to catch the owl."

부자는 어린 총각을 집 안으로 맞이했어요.

The rich man greeted the young bachelor into the house.

그런데 활을 가져오지 않고
빈 손으로 온 것을 보고
이상하게 생각했어요.

어린 총각은 당당하게 말했어요.

"부엉이를 잡는 것은 활이 필요 없는
아주 간단한 일입니다."

부자는 어린 총각을 한 번
믿어보기로 했어요.

어린 총각은 늦은 밤까지 기다렸어요.
모두가 잠든 밤, 어린 총각은 사과나무에
조심스럽게 올라갔어요.
나무 위에서 한참을 가만히 기다렸어요.

얼마 후, 멀리서 부엉이가 사과나무를 향해
날아왔어요! 어린 총각은 부엉이가
나무에 앉기를 기다렸어요.
그리고 부엉이의 다리를 꽉 잡았어요.

어린 총각은 나무에서 내려와
큰소리로 외쳤어요.

"부엉이를 잡았습니다!"

부자는 마당으로 뛰어나와서
어린 총각의 손에 잡힌 부엉이를 보았어요.

"고맙네! 자네는 내 사위일세!"

활을 쏘지 못하는 어린 총각은 머리를 써서
결혼도 하고, 부자가 되어서 행복하게 살았어요.

But he thought it was strange to see that he
came empty-handed without
bringing a bow.

"Catching an owl is a very simple task that
doesn't require a bow."

The young bachelor said proudly,

The rich man decided to trust the young
bachelor.

The young bachelor waited until late at night.
On the night everyone was asleep, the young
bachelor carefully climbed the apple tree. He
waited a long time on the tree.

Soon after, an owl flew toward the apple tree
from afar! The young bachelor waited for the
owl to sit on the tree. And he grabbed the
owl's leg tightly.

The young bachelor came down from the tree
and shouted loudly.

"I caught the owl!"

The rich man rushed out to the yard and saw
the owl in the young bachelor's hand.

"Thank you! You're my son-in-law!"

The young bachelor, who couldn't shoot a
bow, used his brain to get married and lived
happily ever as a rich man.

Culture Note

Vocabulary

사과나무 apple tree. 검은 black. 부엉이 an owl. 종이 paper.

담벼락 the wall of a (stone) fence. 반 half. 성공하다 to succeed.

글 (a piece of) writing/text. 쏘다 to shoot. 현명하다 is wise.

자신만만 is full of confidence. 두드리다 to knock/tap.

맞이하다 to greet/welcome. 빈 empty. 손 hand.

당당하게 confidently/in a dignified manner. 간단한 simple.

가만히 steadily/idly. 꽉 tightly.

자네 Formal way of saying "you", from an older to a younger person.

Proverb

사람이 많으면 길이 열린다.
(Literal) When there are many people, a road opens.
If you combine people's wisdom and strength, you can find a way to do anything.

Reading Comprehension Quiz

According to the story, people died because of the apple tree.

A. True B. False

According to the story, the rich man cared for his family.

A. True B. False

Based on the story, the rich man's daughter wasn't married.

A. True B. False

The young bachelor was smart because he had never practiced shooting a bow before.

A. True B. False

Based on the story, all other bachelors tried to catch the owl by shooting a bow.

A. True B. False

The old man decided to trust the young bachelor because he was…

A. Rich B. Good looking C. Confident D. Logical

Based on the story, the young bachelor knew how to climb a tree.

A. True B. False

Answer : B / A / A / B / A / C / A

호랑이가 준 보자기
The Wrapping Cloth the Tiger Gave

옛날 옛적, 가난한 총각이
산 속에 혼자 살고 있었습니다.

Once upon a time, a poor bachelor
lived alone in the mountains.

가난한 총각은 허름한 오두막집에서
살았습니다. 그는 너무나 가난해서,
변소조차 없었습니다.

The poor bachelor lived in a shabby cabin.
He was so poor that he didn't even have a
toilet.

그래서 추운 겨울이 되면
그냥 뒷문을 열고 산에 오줌을 누었습니다.

So in the cold winter, he'd just open the back
door and pee in the mountain.

어느 날, 산신령이 그 모습을 보고
크게 노하였습니다.

One day, the mountain spirit was very angry
when he saw it.

그래서 산에 사는 호랑이를 불러서
총각을 혼내주라고 명령했습니다.

So he called a tiger living in the mountain and
ordered it to scold the bachelor.

호랑이는 어두운 밤에 총각의 집으로
몰래 내려왔습니다.

The tiger sneaked down to the bachelor's
house on a dark night.

그리고 변소 뒤에서
총각이 나오기를 기다렸습니다.

And he waited behind the toilet for the
bachelor to come out.

아니나 다를까, 그날도,
총각은 산에 오줌을 누었습니다.

Sure enough, that day too, the bachelor peed in
the mountain.

호랑이가 달려가 총각을 혼내주려 했지만,
총각이 중얼거리는 소리를 들었습니다.

"아유, 추워. 나는 집이 있어서 괜찮지만,
집도 없이 산에 사는 호랑이는 얼마나 추울까?"

총각의 말을 듣게 된 호랑이는
차마 총각을 해칠 수 없었습니다.

호랑이는 마음을 바꾸어 산신령에게
자초지종을 말했습니다.

산신령도 총각의 마음에 감탄 했습니다.
호랑이는 산신령에게 부탁했습니다.

"그 총각이 조금 무례하긴 하지만
마음씨는 무척 착한 것 같습니다.
하지만 너무 가난한 것 같은데
총각을 좀 도와주었으면 좋겠습니다."

산신령은 호랑이에게 총각에게 갖다주라며
보자기 하나를 주었습니다.

호랑이는 총각이
자신을 겁낼 것을 걱정했습니다.

그래서 총각이 지나다니는 길목에
보자기를 슬쩍 내려두었습니다.

이튿날, 총각이 일하러 가던 길에
보자기를 발견하고 주워가기로 했습니다.

'이 보자기를 어디에 쓸까?'

The tiger ran and tried to scold the bachelor,
but he heard the bachelor muttering.

"Oh, it's cold. I'm fine because I have a
house, but how cold would it be for a tiger
living in a mountain without even a house?"

The tiger, who heard the bachelor, could not
bear to harm the bachelor.

The tiger changed its mind and told the
mountain spirit the whole story.

The mountain spirit also admired the
bachelor's heart. The tiger asked the
mountain spirit,

"The bachelor is a little rude, but he seems
to have a very nice heart. But I think he's too
poor, so I hope you can help the bachelor."

The mountain spirit gave the tiger a
wrapping cloth to take to the bachelor.

The tiger was worried that the bachelor
would be afraid of him.

So he put down the wrapping cloth on the
path where the bachelor passed by.

The next day, the bachelor found a wrapping
cloth on his way to work and decided to pick
it up.

Where should I use this cloth?

생각하던 총각은 날씨가 추워서
보자기를 머리에 둘렀습니다.

보자기를 두르고 길을 가는데
정말 이상한 일이 일어났습니다.

어디선가 말소리가 들렸습니다.
귀를 기울이니 나무 위의 참새가
사람처럼 말을 하고 있었습니다!

그 보자기가 바로
요술보자기 였던 것이었습니다.

놀란 총각은 가만히
참새의 말에 귀를 기울였습니다.

“얘들아, 옆 마을 부자 영감 딸이
병에 걸려 죽어간데. 그 집 지붕에에 사는
천년 먹은 지네 때문에 그런 건데
사람들은 전혀 모른데.”

“그러게. 지붕을 들어내고 지네를 죽이면
딸의 병도 나을 텐데…”

그 말을 들은 총각은 당장 지게를 벗어 던지고
부자 영감의 집으로 향했습니다.

“내가 이 집 딸을 살려줄 테니
큰 사다리 하나와 담배,
그리고 부싯돌을 갖다주십시오.”

부자 영감은 당장 총각이 말한 것들을
가져다주었습니다.

The bachelor who was thinking, put it around his head because the weather was cold.

Something really strange happened as he was walking on the street with the wrapping cloth on.

He heard a sound of speech from somewhere. Listening carefully, it was the sparrow on the tree talking like a human!

The wrapping cloth was a magic cloth.

The surprised bachelor listened carefully to the sparrow.

"Guys, the daughter of the rich old man in the next village is dying of illness. It's because of the centipede who lived on the roof of the house for a thousand years, but people have no idea."

"I know. If you take out the roof and kill the centipede, the daughter's illness will be cured..."

Upon hearing that, the bachelor immediately threw off his back carrier and headed to the rich old man's house.

"I'll save the daughter of this family, so please bring me a big ladder, a cigarette, and a flint."

The rich old man immediately brought the things the bachelor said.

총각은 담배와 부싯돌을 들고
사다리를 타고 지붕으로 올라갔습니다.

총각이 지붕에 올라가 지붕을 들어내니
커다란 지네 한 마리가 꿈틀거리고 있었습니다.

총각이 부싯돌로 담배에 불을 붙였습니다,
그리고 지네에게 연기를 내뿜었더니
지네가 땅에 떨어져 죽었습니다.

총각은 부자 영감 딸의 목숨을 살렸습니다.

부자집에는 잔치가 벌어졌습니다.
부자 영감은 총각을 사위로 삼았습니다,

총각은 부자 영감의 외동딸과
행복하고 부유하게 오래오래 살았습니다.

The bachelor climbed up the roof on a
ladder with a cigarette and flint.

When the bachelor climbed up to the roof
and lifted the roof, a large centipede was
wriggling.

The bachelor lit a cigarette with a flint, and
when he puffed out smoke at the centipede,
the centipede fell to the ground and died.

The bachelor saved the life of the daughter
of the rich old man.

A feast was held at the rich family's home.
The rich old man took the bachelor as his
son-in-law.

The bachelor lived happily and richly with
the only daughter of the rich old man.

Culture Note

Vocabulary

허름한 shabby. 변소 a toilet. 조차 even. 뒷문 backdoor. 오줌 pee.

혼내주다 to scold. 명령하다 to order/command. 아니나 다를까 sure enough.

중얼거리다 to mumble. 차마 (cannot) bear to. 감탄하다 to admire/awe.

부탁하다 to ask a favor. 조금 a little. 무례하다 rude/impolite/insolent.

보자기 wrapping cloth. 지나다니다 to pass through. 길목 a street corner.

슬쩍 stealthily/secretly. 이튿날 the next day. 날씨 weather. 이상한 strange.

참새 a sparrow. 요술 magic/witchcraft. 귀를 기울이다 to listen carefully.

지네 a centipede. 지게 a back carrier. 사다리 a ladder. 담배 tobacco.

부싯돌 a flint. 꿈틀거리다 to wriggle. 불을 붙이다 to light a fire. 연기 smoke.

내뿜다 to puff out/spout/spew. 사위 son-in-law.

~로 삼다 to take (someone) as ~. 외동딸 an only daughter. 부유하게 richly/affluently.

Proverb

사나운 개도 먹여 주는 사람은 안다
(Literal) Even fierce dogs recognize who feeds them.
Not recognizing a grateful person makes you less than a beast.

Reading Comprehension Quiz

According to the story, we can assume that the bachelor was living alone because he was poor.

A. True B. False

According to the story, his house didn't have a bathroom because he couldn't afford it.

A. True B. False

Based on the story, peeing in the mountain is something the mountain spirit doesn't like.

A. True B. False

The tiger couldn't hurt the bachelor because…

A. The tiger never hurt anyone before. B. The bachelor had to support his family.
C. The tiger had human friends. D. The bachelor was kind-hearted.

Based on the story, we can assume that the tiger and the mountain spirit are also compassionate.

A. True B. False

According to the story, the bachelor put the wrapping cloth around his head because the tiger told him to do so.

A. True B. False

According to the story, the most likely cause of the rich old man's daughter's mysterious illness was…

A. The centipede B. The cigarette smoke C. The wrapping cloth D. The roof

Answer : B / A / A / D / A / B / A

효녀 심청
The Filial Daughter Shimcheong

옛날 어느 마을에
심봉사 라고 불리는 장님이 있었습니다.

Once upon a time, there was a blind man called Shimbongsa in a village.

그에게는 심청이라는
착하고 이쁜 딸이 있었습니다.

He had a kind and pretty daughter named Shimcheong.

심청이는 장님인 아버지를 위해
열심히 일했습니다.

Shimcheong worked hard for her blind father.

그뿐만 아니라, 심청이는 아버지를
사랑으로 보살폈습니다.

Not only that, Shimcheong took care of her father with love.

어느 날 심봉사는 아버지를 위해 힘들게 사는
딸이 불쌍하게 느껴졌습니다.

One day, Shimbongsa felt sorry for his daughter, who was having a hard life for her father.

그래서 심봉사는 딸에게
도움이 되고 싶었습니다.

So, Shimbongsa wanted to be helpful to his daughter.

심봉사는 돈을 벌기 위해 집을 떠났습니다.

Shimbongsa left home to make money.

안타깝게도 그는 눈이 보이지 않아
개울에 빠졌습니다.

Unfortunately, he fell into a stream because he couldn't see.

이걸 본 한 스님이 그를 구해주었습니다.

A monk who saw this saved him.

스님은 쌀 삼백석을 시주하면
심봉사가 다시 앞을 볼 수 있다고 했습니다.

The monk said if he donates three hundred bags of rice, he could see again.

심봉사는 다시 앞을 볼 수 있다는 기쁨에
스님과 약속을 했습니다.

Shimbongsa made a promise to the monk out
of joy that he could see again.

하지만 곧 후회했습니다.

But he soon regretted it.

심봉사는 가난해서
쌀 삼백석을 공양할 돈이
없었기 때문이었습니다.

It's because Shimbongsa was poor
and didn't have money to donate
three hundred bags of rice.

심청이가 걱정하는 아버지의 얼굴을 보고서
이유를 물었습니다.

Shimcheong saw her father's worried face and
asked why.

이유를 알게 된 심청이는
아버지를 돕고 싶었습니다.

Simcheong, who learned the reason,
wanted to help her father.

때마침 심청이는
외국의 상인들이 무역하기 위해
조선에 왔다는 소식을 들었습니다.

Just in time, Shimcheong heard that foreign
merchants came to Joseon to trade.

그들은 인당수를 건너야 했지만,
물살이 너무 험해서
오랫동안 멈춰 있었습니다.

They had to cross the Indangsu River, but the
current was so rough that they stopped for a
long time.

어쩔 수 없이 그들은 바다의 용왕님께
어린 처녀를 제물로 바치기로 했습니다.

Inevitably, they decided to sacrifice a young
maiden to the Dragon King of the Sea.

이 이야기를 들은 심청이는 쌀 삼백석에
자신을 희생하기로 했습니다.

Upon hearing this story, Shimcheong decided
to sacrifice herself for
three hundred bags of rice.

물론 심청이는 아버지에게는 말하지 않았습니다.

Of course, Shimcheong didn't tell her father.

심청이는 떠나기 전날
아버지께 맛있는 음식을 만들어 드렸습니다.

Shimcheong made delicious food for her
father the day before she left.

심청이는 쌀 삼백석을 공양했습니다.

Shimcheong donated
three hundred bags of rice.

하지만 안타깝게도,
스님은 약속을 지키지 않았습니다.

Unfortunately, however, the monk did not
keep his promise.

심청이는 상인들의 어선을 타고 가서
인당수로 몸을 던졌습니다.

Shimcheong went on a merchant's fishing boat
and threw herself into the Indangsu River.

바닷물에 빠진 심청이는 정신을 잃었습니다.

Shimcheong, who fell into the sea, lost
consciousness.

놀랍게도 심청이는 그곳에서
용왕님을 만났습니다.

Surprisingly, Shimcheong met the Dragon
King there.

용왕님은 심청이의 이야기를 들었습니다.

The Dragon King heard Shimcheong's story.

용왕님은 심청이를
커다란 연꽃에 태워서
바다 위로 띄워 주었습니다.

The Dragon King put Shimcheong on a large
lotus flower and floated her above the sea.

물 위로 떠 오른 심청이는
바다를 지나가던 왕의 눈에 띄어 결혼하여
왕비가 되었습니다.

Shimcheong, who floated on the water, caught
the eyes of the king passing by the sea and
married and became a queen.

왕비가 된 심청이는
아버지를 생각하면 항상 슬펐습니다.

Shimcheong, who became a queen, was
always sad when she thought of her father. So

그래서 심청이는 왕에게 요청하여
전국의 봉사를 초청하는 잔치를 열었습니다.

Shimcheong asked the king to hold a feast to
invite the blind from all over the country.

마침내 심청이는 아버지를 찾았습니다.

Finally, Shimcheong found her father.

심청이는 아버지를 보자마자
아버지를 불렀습니다.

As soon as Shimcheong saw her father, she
called to her father.

심봉사는 죽은 줄 알았던 딸의 목소리에
깜짝 놀랐습니다.

Shimbongsa was surprised by the voice of her
daughter whom he thought was dead.

그리고 그 놀라움에 심봉사는 눈을 떴습니다.

심청이와 아버지는 오래오래 행복하게
잘 살았다고 합니다.

And with that surprise, Shimbongsa opened
his eyes.

Shimcheong and her father are said to have
lived happily for a long time.

Culture Note

The tale of Simcheong is one of the most beloved Korean folk tales. It's also been made into pansori, a Korean opera. Through this story, you can see how much Koreans regard filial piety as an important value. Through the sacrifice of her life for her father and the reaction of the Dragon King, who is moved by her kind heart, we can also see that filial piety toward parents is a value that all members of Korean society share, including the mythical beings.

Vocabulary

봉사 (formal) a blind person. 심봉사 literally means "Shim the Blind".

장님 (informal) a blind person. 이쁜 pretty/beautiful. It's a variation of 예쁜.

보살피다 to look after someone. 도움 a help/support. 돈을 벌다 to make/earn money. 안타깝게도 unfortunately/regrettably. 개울 a brook/stream.

때마침 just in time. 외국 overseas. 상인 a merchant. 무역 a trade.

조선 the old kingdom of Korea (1392-1897). 건너다 to cross (a river).

물살 the current of water. 험하다 rugged/dangerous. 제물 offering/sacrifice.

공양하다 to offer/donate. 어선 a fishing boat. 연꽃 a lotus flower.

눈에 띄다 catch someone's eye. 왕비 a queen. 전국 the entire nation.

하나뿐 only one.

Proverb

효성이 지극하면 돌 위에 풀이 난다.
(Literal) Extremely devoted filial piety makes grass grow even on a stone.
It means that if filial piety is sincere, even heaven will be moved and show a miracle.

Reading Comprehension Quiz

According to the story, it's not clear why Simbongsa became blind.

A. True. B. False

Based on the story, Simcheong looked after his father with love because she also had a disability.

A. True B. False

Simbongsa wanted to help her daughter by...

A. Helping her with her work. B. Making money.
C. Submitting a petition. D. Finding her a better-paying job.

A monk saved Simbongsa because he wanted to have three hundred bags of rice.

A. True B. False

Simbongsa soon regretted making a promise with the monk because...

A. He doesn't believe in the teachings of Buddha.
B. He didn't want to be able to see again.
C. He didn't have enough money.
D. He misunderstood the monk's offer.

Simcheong didn't tell her father about her plan because she thought that...

A. The monk would change his mind. B. The magistrate wouldn't allow it.
C. Her father would take all the money. D. Her father would be deeply worried.

SImbongsa was surprised to hear her daughter's voice because...

A. It was different from what she used to sound like.
B. He didn't know where he was.
C. He couldn't see what was in front of him.
D. He thought she was dead.

Answer : A / B / B / B / C / D / D

부자집의 며느리뽑기
How the Rich Family Picked Their Daughter-In-Law

옛날에 어느 마을에 부자가 살고 있었습니다.
하나뿐인 그의 아들이
혼인할 나이가 되었습니다.

Once upon a time, there was a rich man living in a village. His only son became old enough to marry.

그래서 부자는 성실하고 검소한 며느리를
찾기 시작했습니다.

So the rich man began looking for a sincere and frugal daughter-in-law.

부자는 특별한 시험을 통해 며느리를
뽑기로 했습니다.

The rich man decided to pick a daughter-in-law through a special test.

그 시험은 쌀 한 자루,
콩 한 자루로 한 달을 생활하는 것이었습니다.

The test was to live a month with a bag of rice and a bag of beans.

부인은 걱정했지만, 부자는 현명한 처녀라면
굶어 죽지 않으리라 생각했습니다.

The wife was worried, but the rich man thought that a wise maiden wouldn't starve to death.

그 후로 삼년 동안
마을의 많은 처녀가 다녀갔습니다.
하지만 누구도 일주일을 버티지 못했습니다.

For the next three years, many maidens of the village visited. But no one could last a week.

"영감, 이제 시험은 그만 하는 것이 좋겠어요."
부인은 다시 말했습니다.

"Honey, you'd better stop the test now," the wife said again.

그러던 어느 날, 어린 처녀가
부자를 찾아왔습니다.

Then one day, a young maiden came to see the rich man.

어린 처녀가 온 첫날,
부인은 어린 처녀에게 물어보았습니다.

"처녀는 여기 언제까지 있을 예정인가?"

어린 처녀는,

"한 달을 지내고 이 집 며느리가 되어야지요."
하고 대답했습니다.

그날 저녁, 밥을 지으러 부엌에 들어간
어린 처녀는
쌀과 콩을 듬뿍듬뿍 퍼냈습니다.

이것을 걱정한 부인은,

"그렇게 쌀과 콩을 생각없이 먹으면
사흘밖에 버틸 수 없어요"
하며 어린 처녀를 말렸습니다.

그러자 어린 처녀는,

"사흘을 먹더라도 넉넉히 먹어야지요.
제가 밥을 지을 테니 같이 먹어요."
라고 대답했습니다.

부인의 말대로 사흘이 지나자
쌀과 콩은 모두 동이 났습니다.

그러자 어린 처녀가 말했습니다.

"오늘부터는 일해서 먹고 살아야겠으니
일감을 구해 주세요. 어떤 일이라도 좋아요."

On the first day of the young maiden's arrival,
the wife asked the young maiden.

"Young lady, how long will you be here?"

The young maiden replied,

"I'll stay for a month
and be the daughter-in-law of this house."

That evening, the young maiden who went
into the kitchen to cook rice,
scooped out plenty of rice and beans.

Worried about this, the wife stopped the
young maiden, saying,

"If you eat rice and beans without thinking,
you can only last three days."

Then the young maiden said,

"Even if you eat for three days, you have to eat
plenty. I'll cook rice, so let's eat together."

As the wife said,
they ran out of rice and beans three days later.

Then the little maiden said,

"From today onwards, I'll have to work and
make a living, so please find work for me.
Anything is fine."

부인은 어린 처녀의 밝고 씩씩한 태도에
놀랐습니다.

기분이 좋아진 부인은
부자에게 달려가 이 사실을 말했습니다.

"일을해서 먹고 살겠다고 했다고?
기특한 처녀일세."

부자는 기뻐했습니다.

그날 이후로 어린 처녀는
부인이 받아온 바느질 일을 열심히 했습니다.

어린 처녀의 뛰어난 바느질 솜씨는
마을에 금방 알려졌습니다.

창고에는 바느질삯으로 받은 쌀들이
차곡차곡 쌓이기 시작했습니다.

한 달이 지나자 창고는
어린 처녀가 벌어들인 일 년 치 양식으로
가득 채워졌습니다.

부자는 기뻐하면서 말했습니다.

"드디어 며느리로 완벽한 귀한 처녀를 얻었소.

이제야 내가 그토록
오래 기다린 이유를 알겠소?

주어진 것에 만족하고
노력하지 않는 사람은 얻을 것이 없지.

The wife was surprised by the young maiden's
bright and brave attitude.

Feeling better, the wife ran to the rich man and
told him this.

"She said she'd work and make a living?
She's a commendable maiden."

The rich man rejoiced.

Since that day, the young maiden
has worked hard on sewing works that the
wife received.

The young maiden's excellent sewing skills
were quickly known to the village.

The rice received for the sewing work began to
pile up in the warehouse.

A month later, the warehouse was filled with a
year's worth of food earned by the young
maiden.

The rich man said with joy.

"I finally got the perfect precious maiden
as my daughter-in-law.

Do you now know
why I've been waiting for such a long time?

Those who are satisfied with what they are
given and do not try have nothing to gain.

하지만 열심히 일하는 사람은
부를 누릴 자격이 있지.

그리고 그것을
의미 있게 사용할줄 알기 때문이오."

부자는 어린 처녀를 며느리로 맞아들이고
더욱 큰 부자가 되어
오래오래 행복하게 살았습니다.

But hard-working people deserve to enjoy
wealth.

And it's because they know how to use it
meaningfully."

The rich family welcomed the young maiden
as their daughter-in-law and became even
richer, and lived happily for a long long time.

Culture Note

Korea is traditionally a paternal society, but women played an important role in the family. The mother managed the family assets and educated their children at home, and that's why people thought it was crucial to have a wise daughter-in-law or wife in the family. The moral of the story is that, rather than blaming the circumstances you are put in, you will get good results if you work diligently, no matter how hopeless it may seem.

Vocabulary

혼인 marriage. 성실한 faithful/sincere. 검소한 frugal/thrifty.

며느리 daughter-in-law. 특별한 special. 시험 test/exam. 쌀 rice.

자루 bag/sack. 콩 bean(s). 생활하다 to make a living.

굶어 죽다 to starve to death. 예정 a plan. 듬뿍듬뿍 plentiful.

퍼내다 to scoop out. 말리다 to stop (someone from doing something).

넉넉히 enough/sufficiently. 동이 나다 to run out of. 일감 a work/job/project.

씩씩한 brave/confident. 태도 attitude. 기특한 commendable/praiseworthy.

바느질 sewing. 뛰어난 exceptional/outstanding. 창고 a warehouse/storage.

양식 (formal) food/provisions. 완벽한 perfect. 그토록 that much.

만족하다 to be satisfied. 노력하다 to make efforts. 누리다 to enjoy.

의미 a meaning. 사용하다 to use.

Proverb

구슬이 서 말이라도 꿰어야 보배다.
(Literal) Even if you have three bags of glass beads,
they become a treasure only when you string them together.
A pearl is worthless as long as it is in its shell.
It means that no matter how good it is, it is valuable only when it is made useful.

Reading Comprehension Quiz

According to the story, the rich man had many children.

A. True B. False

The rich man wanted to have more than one daughter-in-law.

A. True B. False

According to the story, only a few who took the test could last more than a week.

A. True B. False

The wife asked her husband to stop the test because it was too costly.

A. True B. False

According to the story, the young maiden wasn't actually interested in becoming the daughter-in-law of the rich man.

A. True B. False

According to the story, the young maiden was skilled at sewing.

A. True B. False

According to the story, we can assume that the new daughter-in-law helped the family prosper even more.

A. True B. False

Answer : B / B / B / B / B / A / A

개와 고양이와 소원을 들어주는 푸른 구슬
The Dog and the Cat
and the Wish-Making Blue Bead

옛날 옛적 어느 마을에
마음씨 착한 할아버지와 할머니가
살고 있었어요.

할아버지와 할머니는 자식이 없었어요.

그래서 개와 고양이를 가족처럼 키우며
살고 있었어요.

어느 날 할아버지는 강가에서
낚시하고 있었어요.

하지만 물고기는 한 마리도 잡을 수 없었고,
하루 종일 아무것도 먹지 못한 할아버지는
배가 무척 고파졌어요.

집으로 돌아가려고 생각한 그때,
낚시대가 움직였어요!

낚싯대를 끌어 올리자,
커다란 금빛 잉어가 매달려 있었어요.

신비롭게도, 할아버지에게 붙잡힌 금빛 잉어는
눈물을 뚝뚝 흘렸어요.

Once upon a time, a good-hearted grandfather
and grandmother lived in a village.

Grandfather and grandmother had no children.

So they lived raising a dog and a cat like a
family.

One day, the grandfather was fishing by the
river.

But he couldn't catch any fish, and the
grandfather, who couldn't eat anything all day,
became very hungry.

When he was thinking about going back home,
the fishing rod moved!

When he pulled up the fishing rod,
a large carp with golden gleam was hanging.

Mysteriously, the golden carp caught by the
grandfather shed tears.

금빛 잉어를 불쌍히 여긴 할아버지는
금빛 잉어를 다시 물에 놓아주었어요.

다음 날도 역시 할아버지는
강가로 낚시를 나갔어요.

그때, 물고기를 닮은 사람이 나타났어요.
그리고 할아버지에게 자기와 함께
용궁으로 가자고 말했습니다.

맞아요.
할아버지가 놓아준 금빛 잉어는 바로
용궁의 왕자님이었던 것이에요.

바다 속 용궁에 도착한 할아버지는
용궁의 진수성찬을 먹었어요.

그때, 금빛 잉어였던 용궁의 왕자가
할아버지에게 귓속말했어요

"용왕님이 무엇이 갖고 싶으냐고 물으면
푸른 구슬을 달라고 하세요."

잠시 후, 용왕님은 할아버지에게
무엇이 갖고 싶은지 물어보았어요.

할아버지는 왕자가 말한 대로
푸른 구슬이 갖고 싶다고 말했어요.

놀랍게도, 푸른 구슬은
소원을 들어주는 구슬이었어요.

The grandfather, who felt sorry for the golden
carp, put the golden carp back in the water.

Also the next day, the grandfather went
fishing by the river.

At that time, a person who looked like a fish
appeared. And he told the grandfather to go to
the Dragon Palace with him.

That's right.
The golden carp that the grandfather let go of
was the prince of Dragon Palace.

After arriving at the Dragon Palace in the sea,
the grandfather had a sumptuous feast at the
Dragon Palace.

At that moment, the prince of the Dragon
Palace, who was a golden carp, whispered to
the grandfather.

"When the Dragon King asks what you want,
ask for the blue bead."

After a while, the Dragon King asked the
grandfather what he wanted.

The grandfather said he wanted a blue bead as
the prince said.

Surprisingly, the blue bead was a
wish-making bead.

할아버지는 푸른 구슬을 가지고
집으로 돌아왔어요.

The grandfather returned home with the blue bead.

푸른 구슬에게 맛있는 음식을 달라고 하면
음식이 나왔어요. 새 옷을 입고 싶다고 하면
새 옷이 나왔어요!

When he asked the blue bead to give him delicious food, the food came out. If he asked to wear new clothes, new clothes came out!

어느 날, 그 소문을 들은 욕심쟁이 이웃이
할아버지의 집으로 찾아왔습니다.

One day, a greedy neighbor who heard the rumor came to the grandfather's house.

푸른 구슬을 구경하고 싶다는 이웃에게,
착한 할머니는
푸른 구슬을 보여주었어요.

The good grandmother showed the blue bead to the neighbor who wanted to see the blue bead.

하지만 할머니가 잠시 자리를 비운 사이,
욕심쟁이 이웃은 푸른 구슬을 가지고
도망쳤어요.

But while the grandmother was away for a while, the greedy neighbor ran away with the blue bead.

푸른 구슬이 사라지자, 집과 옷은 예전처럼
헌 것이 되었어요.

When the blue bead disappeared, the house and clothes became old as before.

할머니는 엉엉 울며 슬퍼했어요.
할아버지는 할머니를 위로하며
괜찮다고 말했습니다.

The grandmother cried and was sad. The grandfather comforted his grandmother and said it was okay.

개와 고양이는 할아버지와 할머니가
너무 가여웠습니다.

The dog and the cat felt so sorry for the grandfather and grandmother.

그래서 함께 푸른 구슬을 찾기로 결심했습니다.

So they decided to find the blue bead together.

개와 고양이는 욕심쟁이 이웃이 숨어 있는
오두막을 발견했어요.

The dog and the cat found a cabin where the greedy neighbor was hiding.

고양이는 창고에 있던 우두머리 쥐를 잡고,
푸른 구슬을 찾아서 가져오면 살려주겠다고
말했어요.

The cat caught the leader mouse in the warehouse and said it would let it live if it found a blue bead and brought it.

밤이 되자 쥐들은 푸른 구슬을 찾아왔어요.
개와 고양이는 기쁜 마음으로 집으로 향했어요.

At night, the mice found the blue bead and came back. The dog and the cat headed home with joy.

집으로 가려면 강을 건너야 했어요.
고양이가 푸른 구슬을 입에 담고,
개의 등에 탔어요. 개는 헤엄을 쳤어요.

They had to cross the river to get home. The cat put the blue bead in its mouth and got on the dog's back. The dog swam.

강을 건너면서 개는 고양이가
푸른 구슬을 안전하게 보관하고 있는지
물어보았어요.

While crossing the river, the dog asked if the cat was keeping the blue bead safely.

하지만 고양이는 대답할 수 없었어요.
개는 걱정이 되어 계속 물어보았어요.
고양이가 대답하려고 입을 여는 순간,
푸른 구슬은 강물에 빠져버렸어요.

But the cat couldn't answer. The dog kept asking because it was worried. The moment the cat opened its mouth to answer, the blue bead fell into the river.

개는 쉽게 포기하고 집으로 돌아갔어요.
하지만 고양이는 강가에서 계속 기다렸어요.

The dog gave up easily and went back home. But the cat kept waiting by the river.

다음 날, 고양이를 발견한 한 어부가,
자신이 잡은 물고기 한 마리를 주었어요.

The next day, a fisherman who found the cat gave it a fish he caught.

놀랍게도, 물고기의 배 속에는
푸른 구슬이 들어있었어요!

Surprisingly, there was a blue bead in the fish's stomach!

고양이는 푸른 구슬을 가지고
집으로 돌아왔습니다.

The cat returned home with the blue bead.

할아버지와 할머니는 고양이를 아주 예뻐하며
집안에서 키우게 되었어요.

The grandfather and grandmother loved the cat and started raising it in the house.

개는 마당에서 고양이를 마당에서 바라보며
부러워했어요.

The dog stared at the cat from the yard and envied it.

Culture Note

Vocabulary

하루 종일 all day long. **낚시대** a fishing rod. **금빛** golden gleam.
닮은 similar/look alike. **왕자님** a princess. **님** is an honorary suffix.
진수성찬 a sumptuous feast (of food). **귓속말** a whisper. **푸른** blue.
옷 clothes/garment. **자리를 비우다** to step out. **예전처럼** like the old days.
위로하다 to console/comfort. **결심하다** to decide/make up one's mind.
우두머리 a leader/boss. **헤엄치다** to swim. **안전하게** safely.
보관하다 to keep/store. **쉽게** easily. **부러워하다** to envy.

Proverb

다 된 죽에 코 빠뜨리기
(Literal) Dropping a drop of snot in a porridge that was almost ready.
You spoil a good dish with bad sauce.
It refers to the act of ruining an almost completed task by a moment of mistake.

Reading Comprehension Quiz

According to the story, we can tell that the old couple didn't want to have kids.

A. Yes B. No

According to the story, the grandfather became hungry because he couldn't catch any fish.

A. True B. False

Why did the man who looked like a fish ask the grandfather to come to the Dragon Palace with him?

A. To punish him. B. To sacrifice him for the Dragon King.
C. To show gratitude. D. To ask him a favor.

The first thing the grandfather did upon arriving at the Dragon Gate was ask for the blue marble.

A. True B. False

According to the story, both the dog and the cat wanted to steal the blue bead from each other.

A. True B. False

Based on the story, the leader mouse agreed to help the dog and the cat because…

A. The cat threatened to take its life. B. It admired the courage of the dog and the cat.
C. It didn't like the greedy man. D. It didn't understand the value of the blue bead.

According to the story, a fish swallowed the blue bead that the cat accidentally dropped.

A. True B. False

Answer : B / B / C / B / B / A / A

Quick Korean Lessons For Beginners

How To Read and Pronounce Korean Alphabet

	Name	Pronunciation Initial / Final	English Approximation	Korean Example
ㄱ	기역 gi-yŏk	g / k	good	가수 gasu
ㄲ	쌍기역 ssang gi-yŏk	kk / k	skin	꿈 kkum
ㄴ	니은 ni-ŭn	n / n	nano	노루 noru
ㄷ	디귿 di-gŭt	d / t	dog	다리 dari
ㄸ	쌍디귿 ssang di-gŭt	dd	stall	땀 ddam
ㄹ	리을 ri-ŭl	r / l	roman	라면 ramyŏn
ㅁ	미음 mi-ŭm	m / m	man	마법 mabŏp
ㅂ	비읍 bi-ŭp	b / p	bean	보배 bobae
ㅃ	쌍비읍 ssang bi-ŭp	bb	spit	빨리 bbali
ㅅ	시옷 si-ot	s / t	sing	소리 sori
ㅆ	쌍시옷 ssang si-ot	ss	see	싸움 ssaum
ㅇ	이응 i-ŭng	silent / ng	vowel sound	아기 agi
ㅈ	지읒 ji-ŭt	j / t	jam	자유 jayu
ㅉ	쌍지읒 ssang ji-ŭt	jj	hats	짬뽕 jjamppong
ㅊ	치읓 chi-ŭt	ch / t	change	최고 choego
ㅋ	키읔 ki-ŭk	k / k	king	커피 kŏpi
ㅌ	티읕 ti-ŭt	t / t	time	타자 taja
ㅍ	피읖 pi-ŭp	p / p	prize	피로 piro
ㅎ	히읗 hi-ŭt	h / t	home	해변 haebyŏn

	Pronunciation	English Approximation	Korean Example
ㅏ	a	grandpa	자두 jadu
ㅑ	ya	see-ya	야구 yagu
ㅓ	ŏ	up	접시 jŏpsi
ㅕ	yŏ	young	명화 myŏnghwa
ㅗ	o	go	고무 gomu
ㅛ	yo	yogurt	교사 gyosa
ㅜ	u	root	우주 uju
ㅠ	yu	you	소유 soyu
ㅡ	ŭ	good	그림 gŭrim
ㅣ	i	hit	소리 sori
ㅔ	e	energy	세기 segi
ㅐ	ae	tablet	대박 daebak
ㅒ	yae	yes	얘기 yaegi
ㅖ	ye	yes	예복 yebok
ㅙ	oae	where	안돼 andwae
ㅞ	ue	quest	훼손 hweson
ㅚ	oe	wet	최고 choego
While ㅚ is ㅗ + ㅣ so "oi" seems right when followed the rules, but it's pronounced as "oe", and it's not considered a "double vowel", either.			
ㅘ	wa	what	과일 gwail
ㅟ	wi	wisconsin	귀 gwi
ㅢ	ŭi	we	의자 ŭija
ㅝ	wŏ	wonder	권투 gwontu

Pronunciation Rules

Consonant	Name	First Consonant Pronunciation	Final Consonant Pronunciation	Example			When Followed By A Vowel		When Followed By A Vowel 이[i]
ㄱ	gi-yŏk	g		책	book	chaek	책이	chaeg-i	
ㅋ	ki-ŭk	k	k	부엌	kitchen	buŏk			
ㄲ	ssang gi-yŏk	gg		깎다	to carve	ggak da	깎아	ggagg-a	
ㄴ	ni-ŭn	n	n	손	hand	son			
ㄷ	di-gŭt	d		곧다	straight	got da	곧아	god-a	go-ji
ㅌ	ti-ŭt	t		끝	end	ggŭt	끝에	ggŭt-e	ggŭ-chi
ㅅ	si-ot	s		옷	clothes	ot	옷이	os-i	
ㅆ	ssang shi-ot	ss	t	있다	there is	it da	있어	iss-ŏ	
ㅈ	ji-ŭt	j		찾다	to find	chat da	찾아	chaj-a	
ㅊ	chi-ŭt	ch		꽃	flower	ggot	꽃이	ggoch-i	
ㅎ	hi-ŭt	h		넣다	to put in	nŏt da			
ㄹ	ri-ŭl	r	l	말	horse	mal			
ㅁ	mi-ŭm	m	m	솜	cotton	som			
ㅂ	bi-up	b		입	mouth	ip	입이	ib-i	
ㅍ	pi-ŭp	p	p	잎	leaf	ip	잎이	ip-i	
ㅇ	i-ŭng	silent	ng	콩	bean	kong			

Looking at the above chart will help you visually understand how a consonant is pronounced differently, when used as a **first consonant** and **final consonant,** or **batchim.** Note that the colored consonants **retain** their **original first consonant sound** when followed by a vowel. Just think of it this way - a syllable made up of only a vowel always has a ㅇ as a placeholder (we learned this). So, the final consonant of a syllable right before that comes in place of the placeholder. You only need to remember the colored ones.

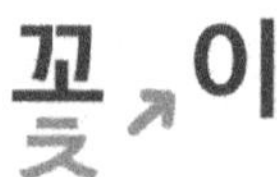

Structure of Korean Syllables

Korean alphabets are then put together to create a **syllable block**, which is composed of a **beginning consonant**, a **middle/final vowel**, and an **optional final consonant**, known as **batchim**. In order to create a syllable block, you need at least one consonant and one vowel. Let's take a look at the example below.

나무 (na mu)

na   mu

Here is an example.

나무 (na mu), meaning "tree".
Let's look at how the word is structured.

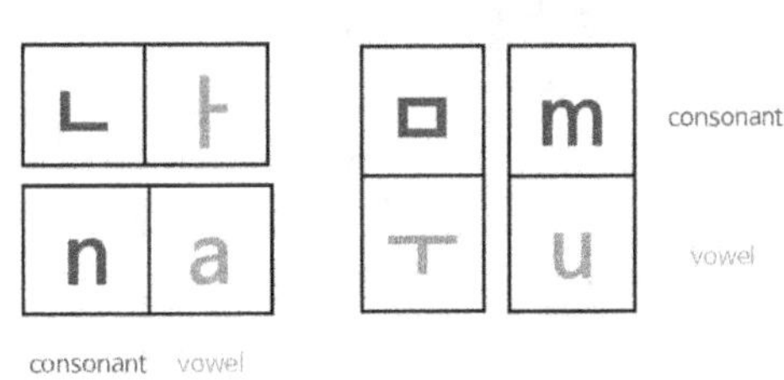

As you can see, a syllable block is composed of a consonant and a vowel. At this point, you might have noticed the position of a vowel is different on the two syllables.

ㅏ	ㅑ	ㅓ	ㅕ	ㅐ	ㅣ	ㅒ	ㅔ	ㅖ
아	야	어	여	애	이	얘	에	예

The 9 vowels above are positioned **to the right side of** a, consonant.
When a vowel is spoken by itself, **ㅇ**, which is silent, is always placed as a place holder.

ㅗ	ㅛ	ㅜ	ㅠ	ㅡ	ㅚ	ㅟ	ㅢ	ㅘ	ㅝ	ㅙ	ㅞ
오	요	우	유	으	외	위	의	와	워	왜	웨

The 12 vowels above are positioned **below** a consonant. Just try to memorize them for now.

As promised, let's talk about **final consonants**, or **batchim.** Simply put, they are the very last consonant character of a word ending in a consonant. For example, the word **"good"** has a final consonant of **"d"**, while the word **"Korean"**has a final consonant of **"n"**. The word **"language"**, however, **does not** have a final consonant because it ends with a vowel. Korean is just the same. See the following to understand better.

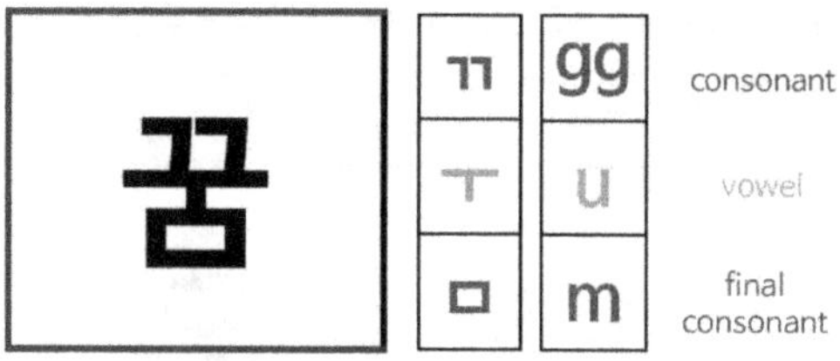

꿈

ggum
("dream")

ㄲ	gg	consonant
ㅜ	u	vowel
ㅁ	m	final consonant

As you can see, the ㅁ comes at the bottom to serve as a final consonant. Notice the vowel ㅜ is placed underneath the consonant ㄲ.

This is the rule we learned just a page ago ;)

Let's take a look at another example to practice.

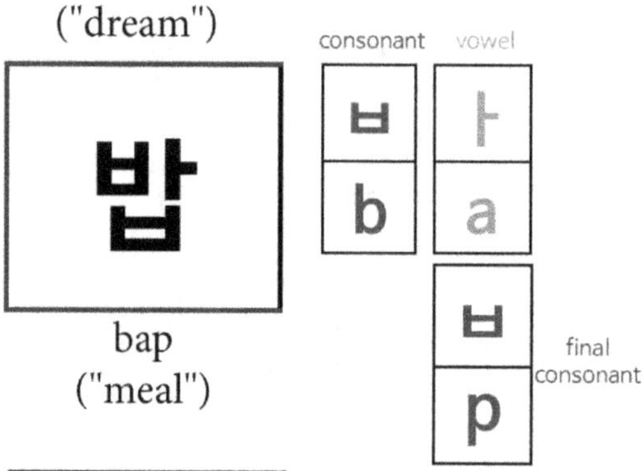

밥

bap
("meal")

consonant vowel

| ㅂ | ㅏ |
| b | a |

| ㅂ | final consonant |
| p | |

In this case, the vowel ㅏ is placed to the right side of a consonant ㅂ, and the final consonant ㅂ is placed underneath the vowel. This is what it looks like.

It's easier to remember like this : **the final consonant is always placed underneath a vowel**, whether the vowel is the right side-type vowel or the underneath type-vowel. Oh, and the word **batchim** literally means "to support/ hold up", so just picture it holding a consonant and a vowel ;)

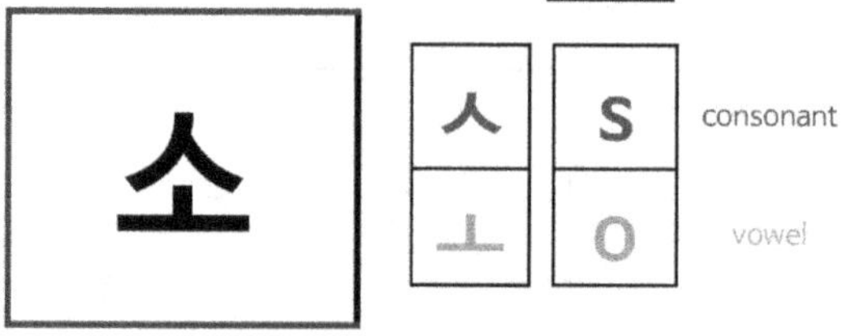

소

so
("cow")

| ㅅ | s | consonant |
| ㅗ | o | vowel |

As a reminder, a syllable that ends in a vowel alone **does not need a final consonant, or batchim.**

At this point, you might be wondering why the same consonant ㅂ, are represented with different alphabet (**b** and **p**). Remember the alphabet chart? We told you that the consonants can be used as a **final consonant/batchim**, and they are pronounced differently when they do. See the chart on the next page.

Structure of Korean Sentences

Now let's get ready to learn the expressions! In order to have a smooth launch, let's familiarize yourself with some of the elements that will keep popping up repeatedly.

First, Korean sentences are structured in the following format.

As you can see, Korean sentences are structured in a different order than English sentences. It should look awkward at this moment, but you will get used to it as we practice more. Another thing you should have noticed is the "는" that comes right after the subject and "를" which comes immediately after the object and an object, left uncolored (we did it on purpose). You will also see that there is no English translation for them, and it's because there aren't any words that correspond to them directly.

This is quite similar to the concept of a/the of English grammar, something that can't be translated directly into Korean, but we know what they are and what they do. Oh, so what are they in Korean?

They are called, **"topic marker (은/는)"** and **"subject marker (이/가)"**

Topic Marker / Subject Marker / Object Marker

Topic Marker

은 (ŭn) **: Used after a word ending with a final consonant.**
Ex.) 몸 mom, "body" + 은

는 (nŭn) **: Used after a word ending with a vowel.**
Ex.) 나 na, "I" + 는

The main role of a topic marker is to indicate what's being talked about (i.e., "topic"), or will be talked about. Although there is no direct translation, you can think of it as meaning "as for".

For example,

하늘은 높다. ha-nŭl-ŭn nop-da : As for the sky, it's high.
*하늘 – sky / 높다 – high

그녀는 학생입니다. gŭ-nyŏ-nŭn hak-saeng-ip-ni-da : As for her, she's a student.
*그녀 – she / 학생 – student

Subject Marker

이 (i) : Used after a word ending with a final consonant.
Ex.) 손 son, "hand" + 이

가 (ga) : Used after a word ending with a vowel.
Ex.) 새 sae, "bird" + 가

In a similar fashion, a **subject marker** comes after a subject to indicate **what the subject of the sentence is**.

For example,

가격이 얼마죠? ga-gyŏg-i ŏl-ma-jyo? : How much is the price?
*가격 – price / 얼마 – how much

자동차가 멈췄다. ja-dong-cha-ga mŏm-chwŏt-da. :The car stopped.
*자동차 – car / 멈췄다 – stopped

Below are some samples from our expressions you will be learning later on. Identify where they are used and try to get used to their usage and nuance.

Now that we covered the concept of **topic marker** and **subject marker**, it's time to talk about "을" and "를", which comes right after the object of a sentence. If you're quick-witted (I'm 100% sure you are!), then you might have guessed the name of this element. Right! It's called the **object marker**!

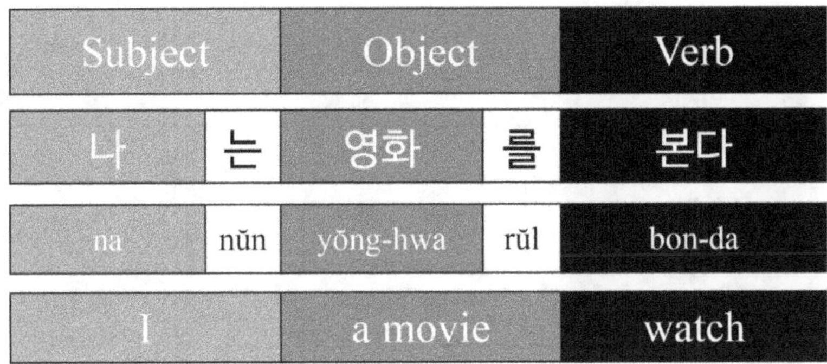

Object Marker

을 (ŭl) **: Used after a word ending with a final consonant.**
Ex.) 수박 su-bak, "watermelon" + 을

를 (rŭl) **: Used after a word ending with a vowel.**
Ex.) 두부 du-bu, "tofu" + 를

Object markers in Korean sentences signify that a noun is acting as the object of the sentence. For syllables ending in a final consonant, use 을, and syllables ending with a vowel, use 를 .

For example,

음악을 듣는다. **ŭm-ak-ŭl dŭt-nŭn-da : (I) listen to music.**
*음악 – music / 듣는다 – to listen

김치를 먹는다. **kim-chi-rŭl mŏk-nŭn-da : I eat Kimchi**
*먹는다 – to eat

In colloquial speech, though, they are often dropped when the sentence object is obvious from the context.

While it's a very confusing/difficult concept for non-Koreans, you shouldn't worry too much about it because Korean people will still understand what you are trying to say even if you mix them up, or forget to use them! Just listen to a lot of Korean expressions and practice by repeating - then you will get the hang of it in no time!

Frequently Used Korean Expressions

All right! Below are some of the most common expressions in Korean.
Knowing these in advance will get you way ahead of others, and help you
easily and quickly identify what someone's talking about. Listen and practice.

얼마	ŏl-ma	how much
언제	ŏn-je	when
어디	ŏ-di	where
누가	nu-ga	who
어떻게	ŏ-ttŏ-ke	how
왜	wae	why
~입니다.	~ ip-ni-da.	It's ~
~입니까?	~ ip-ni-gga?	Is it ~ ?
~있습니다.	~ it-ssŭp-ni-da.	There is ~ / I have ~
~없습니다.	~ ŏp-ssŭp-ni-da.	There isn't ~ / I don't have ~
~있습니까?	~ it-ssŭp-ni-gga?	Is there? / Do you have ~ ?
~없습니까?	~ ŏp-ssŭp-ni-gga?	Isn't there ~ ? / Don't you have ~ ?
~할 수 있습니다. / 없습니다.	~ hal su it-ssŭp-ni-da. ~ hal su ŏp-ssŭp-ni-da.	(Subject) can ~ (Subject) can't ~
~할 수 있습니까? / 없습니까?	~ hal su it-ssŭp-ni-kka? ~ hal su ŏp-ssŭp-ni-ka?	Can (subject) ~ ? Can't (subject) ~ ?
~해 주세요.	~ hae ju-se-yo.	Please do ~ .
~부탁합니다.	~ bu-tak-hap-ni-da.	~ please.
~어때요?	~ ŏ-ttae-yo?	how is / how about ~ ?
뭐예요?	mwŏ-ye-yo?	what is ~ ?
~싶었습니다.	~ ship-ŏt-ssŭp-ni-da.	has/have been wanting to ~
~하세요.	~ ha-se-yo.	please do ~
~해도 되나요?	~hae-do doe-na-yo?	Is it okay to ~ ?

Note On Korean Honorifics

And a few words on Korean honorifics...!

It's well known that the Korean language has a complex honorifics system which reflects the speaker's relationship to the audience. While there are many variants in determining what/when/where/how it's used, the book mainly uses the formal form, because it's the safest bet (no one would frown upon you for being too polite). Below are a few examples.

Informal	Polite	Formal
얼마야? ŏl-ma-ya?	얼마예요? ŏl-ma-ye-yo?	얼마입니까? ŏl-ma-ip-ni-gga?
How much is it?		
공부 했어? gong-bu-hae-ssŏ?	공부 했어요? gong-bu-hae-ssŏ-yo?	공부 하셨습니까? gong-bu-ha-shŏt-sŭp-ni-gga?
Did you study?		
의자야. ŭi-ja-ya.	의자예요. ŭi-ja-ye-yo.	의자입니다. ŭi-ja-ip-ni-da.
It's a chair.		
먹었다. mŏg-ŏt-da.	먹었어요. mŏg-ŏ-ssŏ-yo.	먹었습니다. mŏ-gŏ-ssŭp-ni-da.
I ate.		

While the chart above is y no means a complete list of all the Korean honorifics, you can see a pattern.

* For questions, add ~야/어? at the end for informal, ~예요/어요? for polite, and ~ㅂ니까? for formal.

* For normal, add ~야/다 at the end for informal, ~예요/어요? for polite, and ~ㅂ니까? for formal.

All right guys, now that you've learned the basic elements of Korean, you can fine-tune your Korean with our other titles focusing on different subject matter! Here are some of our best selling titles our readers love.

SPEAKING

LET'S SPEAK KOREAN
Learn over 1,400 Expressions Quickly and Easily w/ Pronunciation & Grammar Guide Marks.

Just Listen, Repeat, and Learn!
Each expression comes with free downloadable MP3 files recorded by a native Korean speaker!

BEGINNERS

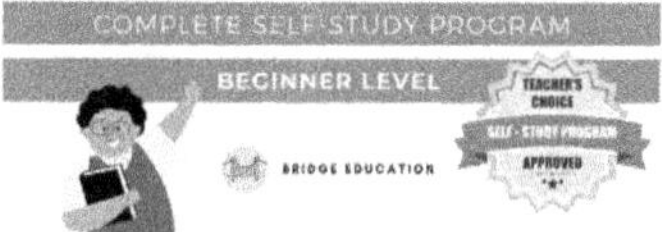

KOREAN FOR EVERYONE
Complete Self-Study Program : Beginner Level: Pronunciation, Writing, Korean Alphabet, Spelling, Vocabulary, Practice Quiz With Audio Files

WRITING PRACTICE

EASY LEARNING FUNDAMENTAL KOREAN WRITING PRACTICE BOOK

GRAMMAR WORKBOOK

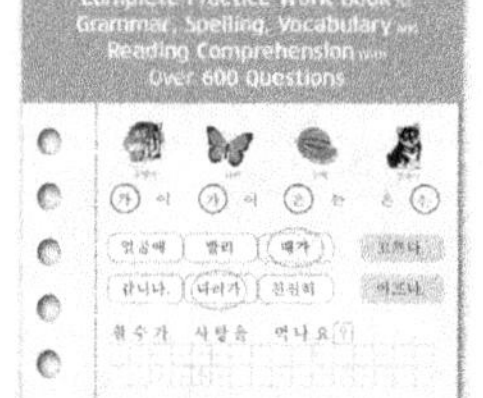

LET'S STUDY KOREAN
Complete Practice Workbook for Grammar, Spelling, Vocabulary and Reading Comprehension w/ Over 600 Questions!

READING COMPREHENSION

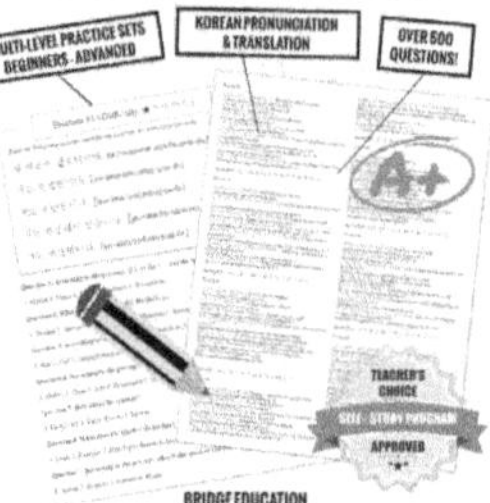

ESSENTIAL KOREAN READING COMPREHENSION WORKBOOK
Multi-level practices for Beginners to Advanced

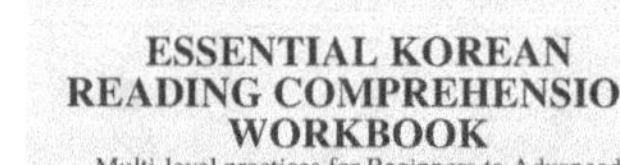

www.ingramcontent.com/pod-product-compliance
Lightning Source LLC
Chambersburg PA
CBHW081254130726
47998CB00010B/2787